SHIPPING AND DEVELOPMENT POLICY

SHIPPING AND DEVELOPMENT POLICY

An Integrated Assessment

Alexander J. Yeats

PRAEGER

PRAEGER SPECIAL STUDIES • PRAEGER SCIENTIFIC

Library of Congress Cataloging in Publication Data

Yeats, Alexander J.
  Shipping and development policy.

  Includes bibliographical references and index.
  1. Shipping. 2. Shipping—Rates. 3. Underdeveloped
areas—Shipping. 4. Underdeveloped areas—Commercial
policy. I. Title.
HE593.Y4   380.5′9   81-4989
ISBN 0-03-059306-9   AACR2

Published in 1981 by Praeger Publishers
CBS Educational and Professional Publishing
A Division of CBS, Inc.
521 Fifth Avenue, New York, NY 10175 USA

Library of Congress Catalog Card Number:
ISBN: 0-03-058651-8

123456789 145 987654321
Printed in the United States of America

ACKNOWLEDGMENTS

To a large degree this book is the result of research completed at the Institute for International Economic Studies in Stockholm where the author spent a year in residence as Visiting Research Fellow. During this period I benefited from a special grant from the Bank of Sweden's Tercentenary Foundation for research relating to the implementation of a New World Economic Order.

My debts to individuals are many and varied. I have benefited from collaborations with Dr. J. M. Finger of the U.S. Treasury and Dr. Gary Sampson of the UNCTAD Secretariat on several earlier works dealing with transport economics. In addition, a joint investigation with Dr. Andrzej Olechowski of the Institute for Foreign Trade Research (Warsaw) forms the basis for the sections dealing with secular trends in transport costs and the differential effects of a cost-insurance-freight versus a free-on-board valuation system. Special thanks are due Dr. Vijay Kelkar of the Ministry of Commerce (India) for comments on the material dealing with India's transport costs. I would also like to express my appreciation to Jack I. Stone, Frank Ramsey, Ho Dac Tuong, and Odd Gulbrandsen of the UNCTAD Secretariat for comments on an earlier version of this work.

Finally, I would like to express my appreciation to the editors of Oxford Economic Papers, Oxford Bulletin of Economics and Statistics, Journal of Development Studies, Bulletin of Indonesian Economic Studies, South African Journal of Economics, Journal of Transport Economics and Policy, World Development, Quarterly Journal of Economics and Business, and International Journal of Transport Economics for permission to quote from portions of articles I published in these journals.

CONTENTS

LIST OF TABLES

x

LIST OF FIGURES

SHIPPING AND
DEVELOPMENT
POLICY

1

TRANSPORT COSTS
AND DEVELOPMENT PROSPECTS

It has become increasingly apparent that most previous analyses of developing country trade and commercial problems provide an inadequate treatment of the influence of transportation costs. While both theory- and practical policy-related investigations recognize that different types of barriers work against developing countries' penetration of export markets, these studies have largely concentrated on the influence of artificial trade control measures such as tariffs or quotas. The neglect of transport costs may have been due to the lack of easily accessible data on their incidence, or the presumption that freight costs were relatively unimportant as opposed to tariffs. Another reason for the relative lack of attention may have been the (erroneous) assumption that transport costs pose a natural barrier and, as such, are largely outside the control of policy makers.

Considerable evidence has now accumulated that shows that these preconceptions concerning transport costs must be reevaluated. For example, most analyses of the liner conference freight-rate-making process conclude that shipping charges are essentially administered prices that can have differential adverse effects on weaker elements. Empirical studies have also demonstrated that, contrary to the assumption often made, transport costs frequently pose a more important trade barrier than most-favored-nation tariffs facing developing country exports to industrial nations. Recent investigations have also shown that the structure of freight rates can have important detrimental effects on developing country industrialization objectives since ad valorem transport costs often rise with fabrication and discourage local processing of raw materials. Nominal transport costs for developing country intratrade have also been shown to assume prohibitive levels with the result that shipping is

a major constraint to any development policy based on collective self-
reliance.*

Aside from the role of these studies in altering the traditional
view of the influence of transport on trade and development, other
factors have made shipping problems of even more immediate direct
importance to developing country governments. In the deteriorating
balance-of-payments position many of these nations find themselves
in today, they have become very concerned with the adverse economic
effects associated with the outflow of foreign exchange for invisibles.
Chief among these transactions are payments for shipping that have
been estimated as absorbing approximately 20 percent of total developing country export revenues. Another factor also adversely
affects the competitive position of developing country exports in foreign markets and the freight costs they bear. Specifically, the incidence (that is, the question of who pays transport costs in a trading
transaction) of freight rates depends on the relative elasticities of
supply and demand for the goods transported. Theoretical analyses
show that the relevant elasticities are such that developing countries
bear a major portion of increased transport costs for both exports
and imports.

Other factors have also heightened developing countries' concerns regarding the influence of shipping on their external commerce.
A major source of friction centers on the contention that liner freight
rates discriminate against specific ports, countries, or products.
In part, such charges originate from the observation of large differences in rates facing similar products transported over alternative
routes. Developing countries have also argued that liner conferences
are insensitive to their institutional needs in failing to offer "promotional" freight rates for new exports. Studies conducted by the United
Nations show that the competitive effects of such promotional freight
rates can mean the difference between success or failure of such
ventures. The geographic pattern of shipping services also poses

---

*The common practice of assessing tariffs on a cost-insurance-
freight (c.i.f.) basis compounds the difficulty developing countries
have in overcoming competitive disadvantages due to adverse freight
rate differentials. Specifically, a c.i.f. tariff valuation base results
in a higher duty collected on a developing country product if these
items experience an unfavorable transport cost differential vis-a-vis
similar products exported from developed nations. Such a situation
would produce a competitive advantage for the industrial country
good due to factors pertaining to both transport costs and tariffs.[1]

major problems as existing liner routes normally tie developing countries to one or a few metropolitan states. These established trade routes may preclude much developing country intratrade since costly transshipment through a commercial center is required. The fact that existing liner routes link developing countries directly to one or a few commercial centers also limits these countries' bargaining power in the pricing of their exports and imports.

TRADE AND FLEET OWNERSHIP

An important element contributing to the developing countries' pessimistic view of their transport problems lies in the imbalance between these nations' participation in world trade and the volume of shipping tonnage actually under their ownership. The fact that developing countries have a small share of the world fleet under their direct control means that a vital factor influencing their international commerce is governed by outside interests. Since foreign shipowners often respond to incentives not directly geared to developing country industrialization objectives, this has led to conflicts between shippers and shipowners. A related issue concerns the extent to which the unfavorable level, structure, and trend in shipping costs could be offset if developing countries had more direct control over the transport services for their exports and imports.

As an indication of the dependence of developing countries on foreign-owned ocean transport, Table 1.1 provides a breakdown of the origins of world seaborne trade in terms of tons loaded in 1976. As shown, developing countries originated 61 percent of total tonnage with the share of developed market economy countries running at about 33 percent.* While these total figures are inflated by crude petroleum shipments, where developing countries originated about 94 percent of world trade, developing countries still accounted for about one-third of total dry cargo loadings.

---

*While developed market economy countries accounted for 33 percent of total loadings, their share of unloadings was 77 percent. In contrast, developing countries had 61 percent of loadings and 19 percent of unloadings. These differences reflect the composition of trade; bulk unprocessed material and petroleum are transported from developing to developed countries, while trade in the reverse direction is largely composed of machinery and fabricated goods.

TABLE 1.1

Comparison of the Origins of World Trade with the Ownership of the World Shipping Fleet in 1976
(all figures in percent)

Fleet Ownership and Origins of World Trade	Developed Market Economy Countries	Open Registry	Socialist Countries	Developing Countries		
				Total	in Asia	in the Americas
Ownership of world fleet						
All vessels	56.5	27.1	8.5	7.5	4.1	2.7
Tankers	56.5	33.7	3.9	5.7	2.8	2.3
Ore and bulk carriers	61.3	29.1	3.7	5.5	3.5	1.9
General cargo ships	46.9	20.0	17.4	14.8	8.5	4.7
Container ships	90.6	6.4	1.4	1.5	1.5	—
Barge carrying vessels	100.0	—	—	—	—	—
Other ships	53.6	7.0	28.4	7.0	3.3	2.7
Loadings in seaborne trade (tonnage)						
All goods	32.8	—	6.1	61.1	37.6	12.1
Crude petroleum	2.4	—	3.7	93.9	70.5	7.3
Petroleum products	30.0	—	12.3	57.7	26.1	27.8
Dry cargo	62.4	—	7.3	30.3	6.5	13.7

Source: Derived from data published in UNCTAD, Review of Maritime Transport, 1977 (Geneva: UNCTAD, 1979).

Table 1.1 also provides information on the ownership of the world fleet that carried this cargo. Shown here is the registration of shipping tonnage by country group in 1976. The figures illustrate the source of some developing country complaints concerning the structure and operation of world shipping. While these nations originate over 63 percent of total trade tonnage, the combined registration of their vessels was only about 6 percent of the world fleet.[*] However, the table indicates that somewhat different patterns of ownership occur within broad vessel classes. For example, the developing country share of the general cargo fleet (14.8 percent) was almost double that for all vessels, while their share of modern container or barge vessels is a negligible portion of the world fleet.

BALANCE-OF-PAYMENTS EFFECTS

Aside from the vast imbalance between developing country trade shares and fleet ownership, further indications of the importance of issues relating to transport can be appreciated by noting the influence on developing country balance of payments. While it may seem surprising in retrospect, little attention was devoted before the early 1960s to the foreign exchange deficits incurred by developing countries for shipping and insurance services. Accurate statistical information on such transactions was lacking and the transport and insurance industries, as well as those developed countries that earned large amounts of foreign exchange from shipping, seemed to have conveyed the impression that these operations were unimportant and unprofitable.

A break from this tradition occurred in 1964 when the first session of the United Nations Conference on Trade and Development (UNCTAD) placed an item concerning invisibles on its agenda. Several preliminary studies on this subject had been prepared, among which was an analysis by the International Monetary Fund (IMF) that

----

[*]Since shipping lines headquartered in developed countries often find that registration of vessels under flags of convenience conveys substantial tax benefits, or is a means of evading strict safety and labor regulations, the figures shown in Table 1.1 understate the actual control of industrial nations on world shipping. While accurate figures are difficult to obtain, it is generally conceded that the United States is the primary owner of vessels in the open registry category while Japan is a close second.

showed that the developing countries' total 1961 balance-of-payments deficit on goods and services was $5.4 billion, and the deficit on merchandise freight and insurance was about $2.14 billion. Of this latter total, freight accounted for $1.95 billion, or just over one-third of the total goods and services deficit. Thus, the IMF study demonstrated that outlays for transport services were a major element in the developing countries' overall adverse balance-of-payments position.

Subsequent improvements in international financial statistics provide considerably more detailed information for analyzing the importance of freight costs in balance-of-payments problems. One way of utilizing this data to illustrate the importance of developing country shipping problems is through comparisons of the value of foreign exchange required for purchases of transport services with total export earnings. Table 1.2 provides such information for 35 selected developing countries in 1977. Also shown are transport payments as a percent of export earnings and the major types of goods exported by each country.

Overall, 18 percent or $6.7 billion of these countries' foreign exchange receipts are required to pay for transport services. However, this overall average is influenced by several countries like Venezuela and Bolivia that have relatively low freight ratios. In contrast, Bangladesh, Ethiopia, Morocco, Togo, and other developing countries must allocate approximately one-quarter of their foreign exchange earnings to transport payments, while 8 of the 35 countries actually have freight payment ratios that reach 30 percent or more of export earnings. Thus, the sizable foreign exchange values involved, coupled with many developing countries' pressing balance-of-payments problems, have been a major factor leading to efforts to control freight rates for developing country exporters, or to encourage the growth of national fleets.

TRADE, TRANSPORT, AND DEVELOPMENT POLICY

As previously noted, any contemporary assessment of the interaction between transport problems and trade and development policy must recognize two essentially negative facts. First, transport costs are a far more important element in developing countries' balance-of-payments problems than is often acknowledged. This point must be fully recognized in any rational planning of new export ventures. Specifically, outward-oriented trade and development strategies may be less attractive than is often supposed if freight payments to foreign shipowners absorb a sizable portion of any gross

increase in export earnings.* Alternatively, realization of the magnitude of the foreign exchange loss associated with the purchase of
required shipping services may accent the need to develop national
fleets in connection with an export expansion strategy.

The fact that international shipping is largely under the control
of outside interests, which need not respond to factors complementary
to developing country industrialization objectives, must also be recognized in formulation of development policy. For example, international organizations such as UNCTAD and the World Bank have
advocated the advantages of resource-based industrialization in developing countries. The reasoning behind such a proposal rests on
the assumption that if developing countries were to increase the local
processing of their domestically produced raw materials, considerable increases in foreign exchange should result. In addition, the
direct and linkage effects of such processing activity could have an
important absorptive effect on the surplus labor that exists in many
of these nations. However, empirical investigations of liner conference rate-making policies strongly suggest that these organizations
escalate their charges according to the value of the product being
shipped. Such pricing practices work against local processing in
developing countries since they establish a cost bias in favor of primary good exports. Thus, if resource-based industrialization is to
be pursued as a viable development strategy, special attention must
be devoted to ways of neutralizing escalating freight rates.

Other examples also illustrate how institutional factors in
shipping may be a key constraint in achieving developing objectives.

---

*Economists often distinguish between outward-oriented ver-
sus import-substitution trade and growth strategies. Essentially,
the latter attempts to stimulate industrialization by erecting high
protective barriers for domestic industry under which it can develop
without excessive competition from foreign firms. However, the
outward-oriented approach specifically suggests that trade barriers
should be kept as low as possible, thereby subjecting the domestic
economy to the stimulating effects of competition with foreign suppliers. Aside from the invigorating effects of such competition, the
outward-oriented approach also strongly suggests that benefits will
also accrue if developing countries aggressively try to capitalize on
opportunities in foreign export markets. Such benefits include scale
effects from larger production volumes, learning effects, improved
communications, and freer access to new technology.[2]

TABLE 1.2

Comparison of Payments to Foreign Carriers for Transport Services with
the Value of Total Exports for 35 Selected Developing Countries, 1977

Country	Major Exports[a]	1977 Value ($ million)		Freight Ratio
		Transport Payments[b]	F.O.B. Exports	
Bangladesh	Woven textiles (34), Jute (24)	119.6	475.8	25.1
Benin	Cotton (16), Oilseeds (8)	26.2	98.4	26.6
Bolivia	Nonferrous metals (44), Natural gas (8)	75.1	640.5	11.7
Cameroons	Cocoa (34), Coffee (24)	142.4	818.1	17.4
Central African Empire	Coffee (23), Rough wood (20)	35.5	104.5	34.0
Chad	Cotton (62), Fresh meat (12)	45.8	106.6	43.0
Congo	Crude petroleum (73), fertilizers (10)	54.2	266.7	20.3
Cyprus	Fresh vegetables (17), Fruits (14)	61.5	304.4	20.2
Dominican Republic	Sugar (63), Iron ore (11)	127.1	780.5	16.3
Ecuador	Crude petroleum (58), Fruit (16)	196.5	1,385.0	14.2
Ethiopia	Coffee (34), Oilseeds (18)	79.3	330.8	24.0
Egypt	Cotton (37), Yarn (12)	406.3	1,993.0	20.4
Gambia	Oilseeds (57), Vegetable oil (31)	10.5	53.4	19.6
Haiti	Coffee (23), Sugar (14)	39.9	138.4	28.8
India	Sugar (13), Tea (7)	587.6	4,676.9	12.6
Jordan	Crude fertilizer (49), Fruit (16)	151.2	249.0	60.7

Country	Products			
Madagascar	Spices (34), Coffee (22)	61.9	388.6	16.7
Mali	Cotton (44), Live animals (17)	42.9	94.4	45.4
Mauritania	Iron ore (64), Nonferrous metals (29)	45.6	182.1	25.0
Mauritius	Sugar (86), Clothing (6)	69.0	307.6	22.4
Morocco	Crude fertilizer (55), Vegetables (7)	358.4	1,284.3	27.9
Niger	Nonferrous metals (61), Animals (19)	43.3	138.4	31.3
Pakistan	Rice (18), Cotton (15)	237.0	1,117.3	21.2
Panama	Petroleum (45), Fruit (21)	84.5	287.0	29.4
Philippines	Sugar (27), Nonferrous metals (10)	356.1	3,074.1	11.6
Rwanda	Coffee (62), Nonferrous metals (18)	24.5	126.4	19.4
Senegal	Petroleum (20), Vegetable oils (19)	68.0	503.1	13.5
Somalia	Live animals (69), Fruits (12)	26.9	71.3	37.7
Thailand	Sugar (14), Rice (13)	525.4	3,455.9	15.2
Togo	Crude fertilizer (65), Cocoa (17)	37.2	140.6	26.5
Turkey	Cotton (16), Fresh fruit (14)	642.1	1,751.3	36.7
Upper Volta	Live animals (36), Oilseeds (28)	28.0	73.5	38.1
Venezuela	Crude and refined petroleum (93)	1,582.0	9,669.4	16.4
Zaire	Copper (54), Coffee (12)	152.7	863.4	17.7
Zambia	Copper (90), Zinc (22)	61.9	388.6	15.9
Total of above		6,606.1	36,339.3	18.2

a Percentage of total exports is shown in parentheses.

b Includes payments for insurance services.

Source: Compiled from data published in United Nations Conference on Trade and Development, Handbook of International Trade and Development Statistics (New York: United Nations, 1979).

9

Lack of appropriate transport facilities have often been a major bottleneck limiting the benefits of regional integration schemes, while the established North-South pattern of liner conference routes has been a major barrier to expanded developing country intratrade and achievement of a policy of collective self-reliance. Increased recognition is also being given to the necessity of transport planning when attempting to formulate development goals or targets. For example, in the early 1970s the United Nations Industrial Development Organization (UNIDO) established the "Lima Target" under which developing countries were to achieve one-quarter of world industrial production by the turn of the century. However, recent investigations show that the magnitude of investments required for ports and vessels to accommodate such an increase in industrial activity are a major constraint to achievement of this target.[3]

SCOPE OF THE PRESENT STUDY

A theme that runs through this book is that perspectives concerning the influence of transport costs on development policy have altered markedly over recent years. A major stimulus to these changing attitudes has been new empirical evidence that greatly accents the importance of transport problems as constraints to trade, industrialization, and growth. This new view also accents the need to formulate an integrated treatment of shipping problems within models of trade and growth. An attempt to provide such an integrated assessment is a basic objective of this book.

As background to the discussion, Chapter 2 examines the influence of secular changes in transport costs on trade and development in a historical perspective. Specifically, recent trends in ad valorem transport costs are compared with those of previous periods. The objective of this analysis is to determine if changes in freight costs have provided the same stimulus to industrialization and growth over recent decades that they did for the periphery economies of the previous century. Furthermore, a partial equilibrium trade model is employed to quantitatively assess the relation between freight rate changes and developing country exports.

Chapter 3 examines existing institutional factors in shipping and how they may not work in harmony with developing countries' trade policies. Special attention is directed to the operations of the liner conference system, although problems in freight markets for tramp shipping, tankers, and bulk carriers are considered. An effort is made to assess the validity of charges of discrimination developing countries have directed at liner operations, and to provide an evaluation of certain conference practices that have been the source of continual conflict with developing countries.

Chapters 4 and 5 examine the implications of evidence concerning the incidence of transport costs on developing country exports. Here, considerable use is made of recent U.S. import statistics that allow separate identification of freight and insurance charges for shipments, by product by country, at very low levels of product detail. In the analysis, attention is devoted to theoretical questions such as effective protection from transport costs and the way in which freight costs act as a barrier to international trade. The situation of the land-locked developing countries is also examined to determine how transport costs influence the trade position of these specially disadvantaged nations.

The book closes with an overall assessment of the influence of transport problems on development policy, as well as ways in which developing country freight costs could be restrained or lowered. While the focus of this discussion often is on the possible use of cost-saving technological improvements—such as the switch to containerized shipping, rationalization of shipping services, or bulking of cargoes—the potential importance of collective action by shippers to provide some degree of countervailing power to the liner conferences is also examined. Attention is also devoted to the nature and magnitude of the benefits that could result from the adoption of a "code of conduct" for liner conference operations.

NOTES

1. For a related discussion, see Alexander J. Yeats, "Tariff Valuation, Transport Costs and the Establishment of Trade Preferences Among Developing Countries," World Development 8 (March 1980):129-36.

2. For a discussion, see Donald Keesing, "Outward Looking Policies and Economic Development," Economic Journal 77 (June 1967):303-20.

3. See in particular, Wassily Leontief, "The Future of World Ports" (New York: Institute for Economic Analysis, Mimeo., no date) for a discussion relating to this point.

2

OCEAN FREIGHT RATES
AND ECONOMIC DEVELOPMENT:
THE HISTORICAL PERSPECTIVE

Empirical evidence clearly establishes that declining transport costs were a major factor contributing to the industrialization and growth of the periphery economics in the eighteenth and nineteenth centuries. For example, in an important study Douglas North showed that a 1910 freight index for U.S. exports stood at less than one-sixth its level in 1820, or about one-half that at the turn of the century (see Figure 2.1).[1] Factors leading to these impressive reductions in transport costs were innovations in shipping, increased utilization of vessels, reduced port time and ballast, more efficient harbor and handling facilities, improved knowledge of winds and currents that speeded ocean transit, and technological changes in sail and steam shipping.*

The secular decline in the cost-of-carriage evidenced in Figure 2.1 was held to provide an important stimulus to specialization and the division of labor on a national and international basis, and the replacement of the relatively self-sufficient economies that predominated in the Western world. North summarizes the influence of the transport factor in noting that

> revolutionary developments in transport were an essential feature of the rapid growth of the western world over the past two centuries. The striking role of the railroad

---

*Somewhat surprisingly, the shift from sail to steam does not seem to have played a major role in the decline of ocean freight rates. North supports this contention by an analysis of the movement of freight rates on different routes during the nineteenth century in conjunction with the timing and substitution of steam for sail.

FIGURE 2.1

Movements in the U.S. Export Freight Rate Index, 1815–1910

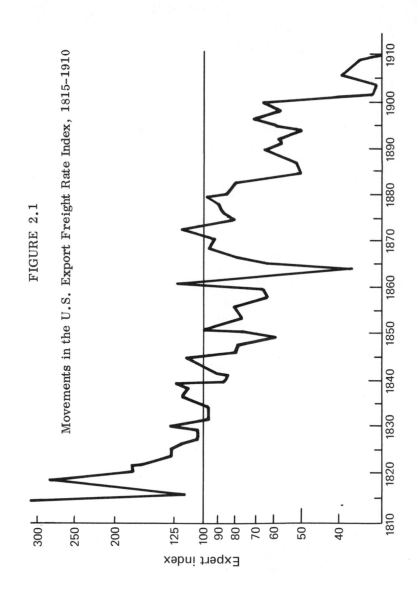

Source: Compiled from data published in United Nations Conference on Trade and Development, Review of Maritime Transport (New York: United Nations, various issues).

in the nineteenth century is well known. However, it
was water transport in which the bulk shipment of commodities began, and it was the development of ocean
shipping that was an integral aspect of the growing economic interdependence of the western world, the opening
up of the underdeveloped continents, and the promotion
of the settlement of the empty lands. The declining cost
of ocean transportation was a process of widening the
resource base of the western world. The agriculture of
new countries was stimulated (and that of the old countries at least temporarily depressed), the specter of
famine as a result of crop failure reduced, and raw materials were provided for industrialization. In short,
the radical decline in ocean freight rates was an important part of the redirection of the resources of the western world in the course of the vast development of the
past two centuries.[2]

While the influence of declining transport costs on the periphery
economies was the primary focus of North's study, changes in freight
costs also had important consequences for the center economies. In
the United Kingdom and Europe, declining shipping costs contributed
to an increase in real wages through lower-priced foodstuffs, while
an increased supply of cheaper industrial raw materials encouraged
investment and the expansion of manufacturing capacity. Thus, a
primary effect of lower freight rates was to redirect European productive resources away from food and raw materials to semifinished
goods and manufactures. It has also been shown that the secular
decline in transport costs resulted in a fundamental improvement in
the terms of trade for European exports, a factor that also contributed
to faster industrialization of the region.

THE INCIDENCE OF TRANSPORT COSTS

When assessing the implications of secular changes in transportation costs, either in the context of the historical model or for
developing countries today, a key question concerns the effects of
these changes on importers and exporters. While transport costs
are formally paid by exporters when goods are sold on a cost-insurance-freight (c.i.f.) basis, and by importers when purchases are
free on board (f.o.b.), the party paying the freight bill is not necessarily the one who bears transport costs. In practice, the exporter
can be said to bear freight costs if the delivered price in the importing
market is not affected by changes in transport costs. Conversely,

FIGURE 2.2

Analysis of the Relation between Supply and Demand Elasticities and the Incidence of Freight Costs on Product Price

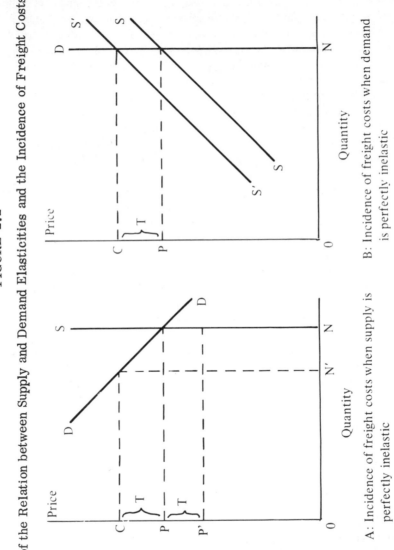

A: Incidence of freight costs when supply is perfectly inelastic

B: Incidence of freight costs when demand is perfectly inelastic

Source: Constructed by the author.

the importer bears the cost of transport if the commodities' price in the export market remains the same irrespective of freight rate changes.

These points can be illustrated through reference to a simple supply and demand relationship. Figure 2.2(A) depicts a situation in which the delivered supply schedule SS for an exportable is completely inelastic with regard to price. In the absence of freight costs, quantity ON would be consumed in the importing market at a price OP. Assuming that freight costs of T per unit are introduced, it is clear that they will not influence the market clearing price. Any attempt to add these charges to delivered prices, necessitating an increase from OP to OC, would be frustrated by a deficiency of demand relative to supply. As a result, excess supply forces the market clearing price back to OP, where the f.o.b. price received by exporters is OP'. Thus, in a situation where export supply is perfectly inelastic, the exporter bears the entire burden of freight costs. It should be noted that if demand is also perfectly inelastic the outcome is indeterminant. The key point emerging from Figure 2.2(A), therefore, is that demand conditions fail to influence who bears freight costs if supply is inelastic; the entire burden falls on the exporter.

Figure 2.2(B) illustrates a situation where an inelastic demand curve for an exportable is matched with a less than perfectly inelastic supply schedule. In the absence of freight costs, quantity ON clears the market at price OP. However, if freight costs of T per unit are again introduced, the supply curve shifts leftward by an amount equal to the transport charge. Thus, SS represents the f.o.b. supply curve, while S'S' is the delivered c.i.f. schedule.* In equilibrium, the market is cleared at the same quantity (ON), but at a higher price (OC), with the increase borne by consumers. Therefore, when demand is inelastic, supply does not influence who bears freight costs. In this situation, consumers in the importing market pay transportation costs or any changes in these charges.

---

*Introduction of freight costs in Figure 2.2(A) does not shift the supply curve since exporters offer the same quantity at all price levels. In other words, the export price is completely demand determined. However, in Figure 2.2(B) freight costs mean that the supply price in the importing market must be higher (by the amount of freight) to continue offering ON if they receive OP. The increase in delivered price (CP), borne by domestic consumers, goes to pay freight costs.

In practice, completely inelastic demand or supply is seldom observed, and these limiting situations are employed solely to indicate tendencies for freight costs to fall on exporters or importers. In normal situations, the incidence of transportation costs on buyers or sellers is determined by respective elasticities of demand or supply. When supply is relatively inelastic, the normal situation for many developing country products, the exporter bears the major part of the freight bill, and the price he receives falls below the "zero transport cost" price by approximately the full extent of shipping costs. It also follows that the fall in the quantity traded below that exchanged in the absence of transport costs is determined by supply. When supply is inelastic, the quantity reduction due to freight costs is small. However, the revenue loss to the exporter may be considerable.

With a relatively inelastic supply, any reduction in the elasticity of demand shifts some of the transport cost burden to the importer. When demand and supply schedules have equal elasticities, shipping costs are shared by buyers and sellers. As demand grows progressively less elastic, the share of freight costs borne by the buyer rises, with elasticity of demand determining the extent to which quantity exchanged falls below that traded in the absence of freight costs.

RECENT EVIDENCE ON TRANSPORT COSTS

In spite of the fact that the role of declining transportation costs in the development and growth process have been examined within the context of historical models, relatively little attention has been devoted to the influence of freight costs on the industrialization of developing countries in the present century. In part, this lack of attention may be due to the presumption that shipping costs are a relatively minor factor when compared to such artificial trade barriers as tariffs. For example, Bela Balassa states that

> the increased emphasis on transport costs and reduced
> emphasis on commercial policy in recent contributions
> to location theory would lead one to expect that transport
> costs have become more—and commercial policy less—
> important in affecting international specialization. In
> fact, the opposite has been the case; since Ricardo's time,
> transport costs have declined in importance while com-
> mercial policy has assumed a greater role.[3]

However, recent empirical studies are at odds with this view. Specifically, Alexander Yeats has shown that the ad valorem freight costs for India's and Indonesia's exports averaged between two to three times the current level of most-favored-nation (MFN) tariffs, while J. M. Finger and Yeats show that ad valorem freight costs have been on a rising trend in the late 1960s and early 1970s (see Chapter 4).

Aside from existing presumptions, another reason for the general lack of empirical analysis may have been the difficulty in securing comprehensive information on the influence of shipping costs on international trade. However, questions concerning the secular behavior of international transport costs are of considerable importance for developing countries today, so an effort should be made to analyze the data that are available. Specifically, if freight costs have not continued to decline through the twentieth century, developing countries do not now benefit from this important stimulus to trade and growth that was enjoyed by the periphery economies of the previous century. If long-term freight costs are in fact increasing, as might be the case if technological innovations in shipping could not offset higher bunker and stevedoring costs, this would have far more ominous implications for developing country trade and industrialization objectives.

Using three separate sources of information, this chapter examines the trend of shipping costs for developing countries' exports. Before beginning the actual analysis, however, the implications of the theoretical discussion (see Figure 2.2) of who bears changes in transport costs should be carefully noted. Specifically, this analysis demonstrated that the question of relative supply and demand elasticities was crucial in determining the incidence of freight costs, and that existing evidence concerning these elasticities was not favorable to developing countries.

In the case of many primary commodities produced by developing countries, short-run supply is generally thought to be quite inelastic due to various factors. For example, many commodities are highly perishable so exporters may be willing to absorb sizable price fluctuations to clear markets. For nonperishable commodities considerable time, and large investments, may be required before production capacity can be raised. Thus, a considerable delay may occur before new mining capacity is developed, or plantation outputs of such items as rubber, tea, coffee, or cocoa can be expanded. Although published estimates of demand elasticities for primary commodities are low, the demand schedules facing a given developing country are likely to be very elastic unless it is an important source of supply, and the

TABLE 2.1

The Ratio of Liner Freight Rates to Prices of Selected Commodities, 1964, 1970, and 1972-75

Commodity	Liner Route	Freight as a Percent of Product Price					
		1964	1970	1972	1973	1974	1975
Rubber	Singapore/Malaysia to Europe	8.0	10.5	15.4	9.2	11.0	18.5
Tin	Singapore/Malaysia to Europe	1.2	1.2	1.6	1.4	1.1	1.6
Copra	Philippines to Europe	11.0	14.0	22.1	9.3	n.a.	n.a.
Jute	Bangladesh to Europe	8.7	12.1	12.6	15.8	18.1	19.5
Sisal hemp	East Africa to Europe	8.4	19.5	18.1	10.0	7.3	12.8
Cocoa beans	Ghana to Europe	3.1	2.4	3.9	3.1	2.3	3.4
Coconut oil	Sri Lanka to Europe	8.8	8.9	14.5	n.a.	7.9	9.1
Tea	Sri Lanka to Europe	6.5	9.5	8.2	10.1	14.2	10.4
Coffee	Brazil to Europe	4.9	5.2	6.7	7.0	8.0	9.7
Palm kernels	Nigeria to Europe	9.5	8.8	16.9	7.2	9.6	25.5
Coffee	Colombia (Atlantic ports) to Europe	4.2	4.2	4.2	3.8	4.8	5.7
Cocoa beans	Brazil to Europe	8.6	7.4	10.7	6.9	6.1	8.2
Coffee	Colombia (Pacific ports) to Europe	4.5	4.5	5.0	4.3	5.4	6.3

n.a.: not available.

Source: United Nations Conference on Trade and Development, Review of Maritime Transport, 1976 (TD/B/ C.4/169) (Geneva: United Nations, March 25, 1977), p. 60.

commodity has no close substitutes. This, coupled with inelastic supply, means that developing country exporters normally bear the major burden of freight costs, and any increase in transport costs may be expected to produce equivalent declines in net export receipts. Stated differently, any increase in developing country freight costs, ceteris paribus, should have more of a depressant effect on exporters' prices than on the consumer price.

The message that emerges from any analysis of the incidence of transport costs is that freight charges have the potential to be of greater concern for developing countries than for industrial nations. As such, questions naturally arise as to the incidence and directional movements of these charges. Some evidence can be derived from UNCTAD sources that monitor freight costs for important primary products shipped along major liner conference routes. Drawing on these data, Table 2.1 shows freight as a percentage of product price for shipments of rubber, tin, copra, hemp, jute, sisal, cocoa, tea, coconut oil, palm kernels, and coffee over the period 1964 to 1975.

On a product-by-product basis, the freight ratios range from under 2 percent for Malaysian tin to a high of 25 percent for palm kernels on the Nigeria-Europe route. Two other products, rubber from Malaysia and jute from Bangladesh, have freight factors close to 20 percent. Since the latter is undoubtedly characterized by inelastic supply and very elastic demand, due to competitive pressures from synthetics and other substitutes, most of the burden of these charges falls on the developing countries.

Aside from the question of levels, Table 2.1 shows that sizable year-to-year fluctuations have occurred in nominal freight rates for certain products. Freight factors changed by as much as 8 percentage points for sisal and 13 points for copra during 1972-73, while a 16 percentage point rise in the freight factor for palm kernels occurred over 1974-75. Analysis of the underlying data shows that wide fluctuations in primary product prices were the main reason for these swings in freight ratios, as conference shipping rates advanced steadily on a secular trend.

Another, perhaps more disturbing, fact emerging from these figures is that a general rise in freight factors seems to have occurred over 1964-75, although it is difficult to separate cyclical factors from trend. However, in every case except one (cocoa) the freight factors for 1975 rose above their 1964 base, often by considerable margins. For jute, rubber, and palm kernels the ratios increased by more than 100 percent, while ad valorem freight rates for coffee were 98 percent above their earlier base. For the 12 commodities, an average increase of 62 percent was experienced in freight factors, with Brazilian cocoa the only item to register a slight decline (down 4.7 percent). One explanation for these relative increases in transport rates centers on the pricing policies of the Organization for Petroleum Exporting Countries (OPEC), which resulted in a four-fold increase in crude oil prices. Since shipping is a petroleum-intensive operation, the increases in crude prices resulted in markedly higher bunker and liner operating costs. Undoubtedly, this was a factor in the dramatic upsurge in shipping rates over the 1974-76.

SECULAR CHANGES IN FREIGHT COSTS: 1938-74

Aside from the UN monitoring of liner conference freight rates, two additional sources of information are available to assess the longer-term incidence of international transport costs. Specifically, the U.S. Tariff Commission conducted a comprehensive survey of ad valorem freight costs for U.S. imports prior to the disruption in ocean shipping that accompanied World War II.[4] Altogether, this study provides detailed freight rate information for over 200 products shipped from specific developed and developing countries. As such, the Tariff Commission survey can be used for estimating the transport cost profile of U.S. imports in 1938.

Recent changes in U.S. import statistics provide detailed current data on international transport costs, with the result that these freight rates can be linked directly to the earlier Tariff Commission study. Specifically, in 1974 the United States started tabulating imports, by product, by country, on a joint free-alongside-ship (f.a.s.) and c.i.f. basis. According to the U.S. practice, the f.a.s. valuation includes the purchase price plus all charges incurred in placing merchandise alongside the vessel at the port of exportation. In contrast, the c.i.f. valuation measures the value of imports at the port of entry in the United States and includes all freight, insurance, and other charges (excluding import duties) incurred in bringing the merchandise from the port of exportation and placing it alongside the vessel. As such, the ratio of the c.i.f. to the f.a.s. value provides a measure of the ad valorem incidence of international transport and insurance charges. These data can be used to estimate ad valorem freight costs for exports of product i from country j (f_{ij}) from

$$f_{ij} = V_c/(V_f - 1) \qquad\qquad 3.1$$

where V_c represents the c.i.f. and V_f the f.a.s. value of exports. Since the import data are available at very low levels of product detail, matched 1974 nominal freight rates can be derived for shipments from those countries included in the earlier tariff commission survey.[5]

TABLE 2.2

Analysis of Changes in Ad Valorem Transportation Costs
for Exports to the United States over the Period 1938-74,
by Country or Region of Origin

Origin of Shipments	1974 Value of Exports to the United States ($ million)	Ad Valorem Freight Rate*		
		1938	1974	Change
All countries	100,030	16.2	14.3	-1.9
Developed countries	60,110	15.9	15.2	-0.7
Western Europe	45,080	17.5	15.8	-1.7
Eastern Europe	420	5.6	10.3	4.7
Japan	12,930	6.4	8.5	2.1
Australia and New Zealand	1,330	4.5	5.8	1.3
South Africa	350	17.6	29.4	11.8
Developing countries	39,920	16.7	12.9	-3.8
Latin America	18,810	18.1	11.4	-6.7
Asia	10,330	16.3	13.7	-2.6
Middle East	5,270	7.7	14.0	6.3
Africa	5,510	17.6	29.4	11.8

*Based on items included in the 1938 U.S. Tariff Commission
sample.
Source: UNCTAD, Handbook of International Trade and Development Statistics (New York: UNCTAD, 1977).

Thus, comparing 1938 with 1974 freight rates shows the change in
nominal shipping costs for specific exports to the United States.

Table 2.2 summarizes the 1938-74 freight rate changes on a
geographic basis, while a separate breakdown shows similar freight
rates for developed and developing countries. The value of U.S.
imports originating in each region, or country group, is also given
to assist in evaluating the importance of these trade flows.

Overall, Table 2.2 shows that ad valorem freight costs for
U.S. imports averaged 16.2 percent in 1938 and 14.3 percent in 1974,

a drop of 1.9 percentage points.* However, the disaggregate statistics show that most of the decline occurred for developing country shipments where freight rates fell by almost 4 percentage points (from 16.7 to 12.9 percent). In contrast, the reduction in ad valorem transport costs for developed countries was less than one-fifth this figure. The table also shows that the developed country decline was concentrated in Western Europe, as other industrial countries experienced increases in ad valorem freight rates.

One important point emerging from Table 2.2 is that the size of the freight cost reductions for developing country exports over 1938-74 were not of the order of magnitude that North indicates occurred for periphery economies during the last century. In this earlier period, a persistent secular decline in ad valorem transport costs was a positive factor leading to trade expansion and industrialization. In contrast, Table 2.2 shows that nominal freight rates had fallen to a level in the 1930s from which further sizable reductions could not occur. Thus, declining transport costs have not provided the stimulus to trade and development that they did for the periphery economies in the nineteenth and early twentieth centuries.

While Table 2.2 suggests that overall transport cost reductions had a relatively minor impact on developing country trade during 1938-74, an important question centers on whether particular product groups experienced important reductions in freight costs. This possibility exists if specialized transport modes, such as bulk carriers or containerized shipping, were especially adaptable to some types of products. If differential transport cost reductions occurred, lower penetration costs may have been a significant factor contributing to the growth of specific industries or export sectors.

Table 2.3 examines the changes in ad valorem transport costs for seven broad classes of goods: foods, agricultural raw materials, crude materials and ores, fuels, chemicals, metals, and other

---

*In 1974, nominal transport costs for U.S. imports averaged about 9 or 10 percent. The fact that the average shown in Table 2.2 is higher is largely because the sample of items upon which these figures are based includes imports that were of key importance in the 1930s. During 1930-70, the composition of imports shifted toward sophisticated manufactures and processed goods; items that generally bear lower freight costs. However, the fact that the 1938 Tariff Commission data are based, to a larger degree, on crude and semifinished products makes the results more relevant to the transport cost experience of developing countries.

manufactures. The table also shows information on the transport cost changes for some of the major two-digit Standard International Trade Classification (SITC) products within each group. Ad valorem freight rates are given for developed and developing countries, while 1974 import figures are presented to help assess the importance of these items in U.S. trade.

Table 2.3 indicates that crude materials and ores experienced sizable reductions in freight rates (approximately 27 percentage points for developing countries), but the transport cost changes for other product groups were relatively small. Fuels experienced the second largest freight rate reduction, about 9 percent, but none of the other major product groups had a transport cost decline that was as much as one-sixth that for crude materials. Related studies by the World Bank and several transport economists suggest that a major reason for the crude material reduction was the development of bulk carriers and compatible loading and unloading facilities. However, these investigations have not considered whether such freight cost reductions work in favor of or against industrialization of developing countries. Greater transport cost savings for crude materials and ores may work against local processing since they reduce the landed cost of these items (relative to fabricated goods) in foreign markets.

To summarize the overall implications of the 1938-74 transport cost changes for developing countries' goods, both observed freight rate changes and import demand elasticities were incorporated in a partial equilibrium import demand model that has been used to assess the effects of reductions in trade barriers.[6] The objective of this exercise was to simulate the change in developing country exports due to the secular change in shipping costs. The results suggest that the freight cost changes that occurred probably increased developing country exports by about 4 to 5 percent above the level that would have occurred in the absence of any transport cost changes. A major factor accounting for the relatively low values for the trade simulations is that the larger freight cost reductions occurred for items with relatively low demand elasticities like primary goods and crude materials.

TRADE AND TRANSPORT COSTS: 1974-79

There is little doubt that the period following the initial 1973 OPEC price action was one of the most unsettled intervals for freight rates and shipping to occur in peacetime conditions. First, the direct impact of the OPEC price increases led many liner conferences to adopt bunker surcharges to compensate for markedly higher fuel costs.

TABLE 2.3

Analysis of Changes in Ad Valorem Transportation Costs for Exports to the United States over the Period 1938–74, by Major Product Groups

| Product Group | 1974 Exports to the United States ($ million) | | Ad Valorem Freight Rate | | | | | |
| | Developing Countries | All Sources | Developing Countries | | | All Sources | | |
			1938	1974	Change	1938	1974	Change
Foods	6,771	11,296	12.5	8.3	-4.2	9.3	9.4	0.1
Meat and meat preparations (01)	338	1,344	5.0	4.3	-0.7	6.2	5.0	-1.2
Fruits and vegetables (05)	747	1,015	13.1	12.0	-1.1	9.3	12.3	3.0
Coffee, tea, cocoa, and spices (07)	2,110	2,298	11.5	8.4	-3.1	10.6	8.8	-1.8
Oilseeds and kernels (22)	31	51	21.0	7.5	-13.5	14.4	10.3	-4.1
Fixed vegetable oils (42)	455	511	14.8	5.4	-9.4	10.4	6.2	-4.2
Agricultural Raw Materials	948	3,587	10.3	14.3	4.0	7.5	11.4	3.9
Hides and skins, undressed (21)	45	156	3.3	8.3	5.0	2.6	4.7	2.1
Crude rubber (23)	517	598	3.6	10.6	7.0	3.6	10.6	7.0
Textile fibers (26)	80	225	9.0	13.5	4.5	6.9	10.4	3.5
Animal and vegetable materials (29)	191	390	14.5	15.7	1.2	10.1	12.1	2.0

Crude Materials and Ores	997	2,276	57.3	30.4	-26.9	65.2	44.5	-20.7
Crude fertilizers and minerals (27)	133	438	41.2	34.8	-6.4	72.9	56.1	-16.8
Metalliferous ores (28)	864	1,838	70.8	26.8	-44.0	54.3	28.1	-26.2
Fuels	19,294	25,350	21.5	13.0	-8.5	14.3	7.7	-6.6
Petroleum and products (33)	19,142	24,210	21.5	13.0	-8.5	21.5	13.0	-8.5
Chemicals	486	3,991	6.7	16.0	9.3	10.4	14.3	3.9
Elements and compounds (51)	288	2,252	4.0	5.0	1.0	5.0	12.0	7.0
Dyeing materials (53)	6	140	8.0	21.5	13.5	4.5	12.3	7.8
Metals	1,734	9,330	10.2	6.8	-3.4	10.0	7.7	-2.3
Iron and steel (67)	561	5,405	39.0	28.0	-11.0	15.1	11.9	-3.2
Nonferrous metals (68)	1,173	3,925	3.0	1.5	-1.5	2.3	1.3	-1.0
Other Manufactures	1,975	8,716	5.2	7.5	2.3	10.1	10.6	0.5
Leather and products (61)	86	185	4.0	7.0	3.0	3.2	6.8	3.6
Textiles (65)	744	1,629	6.3	8.0	1.7	7.3	7.5	0.2

Note: SITC numbers are shown in parentheses. Foods include: SITC 0 + 1 + 22 + 4; Agricultural Raw Materials: SITC 2 – 22 – 27 – 28; Crude Materials and Ores: SITC 27 + 28; Fuels: SITC 3; Chemicals: SITC 5; Metals: SITC 67 + 68; Other Manufactures: SITC 6 – 67 – 68.

Source: Organization for Economic Cooperation and Development, Trade by Commodities, Imports, 1974 (Paris: Organization for Economic Cooperation and Development, 1975).

In addition, the unsettled monetary conditions that also occurred caused many of the conferences to adopt currency surcharges to offset expenses incurred in appreciating currencies. These bunker and currency surcharges coupled with other factors to produce a general upward spiral in freight rates. However, a key question concerning any analysis of freight rate changes centers on the magnitude of these changes relative to those for the traded goods. If transport costs rise at a slower pace than that of the general inflation, the ad valorem incidence of these charges will decline. Constant or declining ad valorem shipping costs have favorable implications for trade as opposed to a situation where nominal freight rates are rising.

Insights into the recent behavior of ad valorem freight rates can be gained from a comparison of movements in indexes of freight rates with similar changes in indexes in import or export prices. As an example, post-1973 changes in the Federal Republic of Germany's liner rate index (perhaps the most widely used international index of liner rates) were compared with changes in import unit value indexes for the United States. While it is difficult to draw firm conclusions from these data, the results suggest that transport costs, relative to import prices, were increasing over the period 1974-79.

In early 1979 the liner rate index had risen 30 percent over its 1974 level, while the U.S. import unit value index rose by about 23 percent. If these figures serve as a guide, freight rates have increased roughly one-third faster than the general level of import prices over 1974-79. While further analysis and monitoring of freight rates is needed, such a development is consistent with the high petroleum component (relative to most manufacturing processes) of shipping and the cost increases that have occurred for this input.

In summary, one key point stands out from the historical analysis of freight rate changes and development prospects. While economists may have had some basis, in the past, for assuming that changes in transport costs would have a beneficial or neutral effect on international trade, the analysis presented in this chapter shows that no such presumption can be made for developing countries today. Indeed, much of the evidence that was examined in this chapter suggests that secular changes in ad valorem transport costs are now moving in an upward direction, thus reversing the downward trend that had its origins in the nineteenth century.

NOTES

1. Douglas North, "Ocean Freight Rates and Economic Development," Journal of Economic History 18 (December 1958):537-79.

2. Ibid., p. 537.

3. See Bela Balassa, "Effects of Commercial Policy on International Trade, the Location of Production, and Factor Movements," in The International Allocation of Economic Activity, ed. Bertil Ohlin et al. (London: Macmillan, 1977), p. 232.

4. See U.S. Tariff Commission, Transport Costs and the Value of Principal Imports (Washington: U.S. Tariff Commission, 1940).

5. For import values tabulated on an f.a.s. and c.i.f. basis, see U.S. Department of Commerce, United States Imports (FT/135) (Washington, D.C.: U.S. Government Printing Office, 1975).

6. A description of the model can be found in Bela Balassa and Mordechai Kreinin, "Trade Liberalization under the Kennedy Round: The Static Effects," Review of Economics and Statistics 49 (May 1967):125-37.

3

INSTITUTIONAL FACTORS IN
SHIPPING AND DEVELOPMENT
POLICY

Any assessment of the influence of transport problems on developing country trade and industrialization must specifically consider the effects of existing institutional arrangements. Indeed, developing countries have maintained that these institutional factors result in serious discriminatory effects against themselves, either singularly or as a group. Developing countries have also alleged that existing institutions result in excessive profits for foreign shipowners, produce a structure of shipping charges that is detrimental to their industrialization goals, or work against their efforts to establish national fleets. Since these allegations strike at matters that are central to current thinking on development policy, the validity of the charges must be examined.

Before attempting such an analysis, however, it should be noted that wide differences exist in the types of markets for shipping services as well as in the institutional structure of these markets. Although an unambiguous distinction cannot always be made, transport economists have found it useful to classify shipping services as falling in three major markets: those for liners, tramp shipping, and tankers or bulk carriers. While the primary focus of this chapter concerns operation of these markets, consideration is also given to institutional factors relating to ports and registration of vessels since these issues have also posed major problems for developing countries.

THE LINER CONFERENCE SYSTEM

Simply stated, liners are ships servicing a given route in accordance with a predetermined time schedule. The routes and timetable may be completely predetermined in that normally no flexibility is allowed except for time lost through accident or bad weather. The exceptions are that route and schedule changes may in cases be allowed so calls can be made at ports on the route if there is sufficient

31

cargo. However, such flexibility would not let the ship depart from the overall route pattern. It should be noted that the most important type of flexibility associated with liners concerns the volume of goods individual shippers can place on these vessels. While alternative types of shipping services, such as tramps, are contracted on a whole vessel basis, liners will accept consignments of varying size even though less than full vessels are involved.

When two or more liner companies service a particular trade route, the competition is invariably limited by agreements covering freight rates and other aspects of competitive behavior. These agreements are known as liner conferences. In practice, internal competition between conference members is normally restricted by agreements covering pricing, the allocation of cargoes and sailings, revenue pools, or the offering of joint services. Some conferences also attempt to resist outside competition by offering deferred rebates or dual rate contracts, that is, agreements giving lower rates to shippers who pledge not to use other shipping services. In addition to these arrangements, many conferences admit new lines only on the vote of existing members. Admission may, therefore, be very difficult or even impossible in the case of some "closed" conferences.*

Within the liner conferences competition is restricted to matters of service with price competition being precluded by the conference agreement. Conferences normally have self-policing arrangements to prevent secret rate cutting or other forms of active competition. For example, in analyzing conference practices to prevent competition, M. G. Valente states that

> the subtle mechanism of incentives, financial advantages,
> and penalties that liner conferences impose on shippers
> effectively restricts the freedom of the latter to choose

---

*Viewed in terms of a limit price analysis, these entry barriers have important effects on the pricing policies adopted by the conferences. For example, the limit price has been defined as the highest common price sellers believe they can charge without inducing at least one additional increment to entry. Thus, the threat of entry can have a moderating effect on established firms' pricing policies. However, the barriers to entry associated with conference anticompetitive practices and restrictions on new members undoubtedly remove some of the moderating effects of the threat of entry on prices. In other words, there is reason to believe that conference prices would be lower if some of the restrictions on new entry were removed.

nonconference vessels. In fact, the effect of the liner
conference practices in limiting shippers margin of
choice is so great that in any study of these practices
the chapter on so called loyalty agreements could be
aptly entitled On Shippers Bondage.[1]

Valente also notes that loyalty to the conference is encouraged by offering a positive financial reward, while disloyalty is punished by
withdrawal of benefits. The inducement to exclusively utilize conference vessels may take the form of a discount or immediate rebate.
Some conferences also adopt dual freight rate systems with the lower
rate for shippers who sign loyalty pledges.

While the characteristics may vary between individual conferences, the UNCTAD Secretariat has attempted to provide a profile
of the common features of these associations and their operations.
This information is summarized in Table 3.1. As can be seen from
the table, the conferences, by various means, have generally adopted
policies and practices that touch on all aspects of developing countries'
commerce. It is precisely these sorts of extensive controls and institutional arrangements that have been the source of friction between
shipowners and developing country shippers. While the conferences
have argued that these institutional arrangements are based on cost-
and efficiency-related factors, they are viewed by developing countries as devices to maintain control over their external commerce.

What freight rate competition that does exist for the conferences comes from two sources: nonconference liners and tramps.
The former operate on the same route as conferences and will generally cut their rates below prevailing levels. Often such competition occurs because the conference has refused the line entry, and a
rate-cutting war may be fought until the nonconference vessel is
either forced out of business or its conference membership is accepted. Vessels of East European countries have been a particularly
strong competitive force on some established liner routes with these
units offering freight rates as much as 20 percent below conference
charges.

THE TRAMP SHIPPING MARKET

In cases where full shiploads are involved, or where shippers
can consolidate cargoes, liner conferences may experience competition from tramp ships. Essentially, the primary difference between
liners and tramps is that the former are servicing regular shipments
over a fixed route. In contrast, tramps are vessels that do not have
fixed routes, but that carry dry bulk cargo over long distances. Some

TABLE 3.1

Tabulation of the Basic Features of Most Self-Regulated Liner Conferences

Feature	Comment
Relations between member lines	
(a) Membership	Closed conference with confidential criteria for the admission, withdrawal, or expulsion of members.
(b) Share of trade	The basis for the allocation of shares of cargo to members is usually kept confidential.
(c) Pooling	Confidential cargo or revenue pooling agreements cover the shares of cargo or revenue due to each member line; sometimes there is provision to ensure the carriage of low-rated cargo.
(d) Sanctions	Agreements provide for sanctions against breaches of agreement by member lines.
(e) Self-policing	Self-policing machinery exists to ensure compliance with the terms of conference agreements.
(f) Publication of conference agreements	The conference agreement is considered as a confidential document.
(g) Contents of conference agreements	Contents of agreements are confidential.

34

Relations with shippers

(a) Loyalty arrangements

Loyalty arrangements comprise fidelity clauses and ties with shippers (dual rate system, contract system, and deferred rebate system).

(b) Dispensation

There are no arrangements for giving reasonably prompt dispensation to loyal shippers to use nonconference vessels.

(c) Publication of tariffs and related regulations

No provision for publication is usually made.

(d) Consultation machinery

There is general concentration of authority at headquarters.

(e) Representation

There is no representation of merchant interests in rates and other conference committees.

Freight rates

(a) General freight rate increases

Freight rates are imposed unilaterally; the basis for freight rate changes is confidential. There are usually no specific provisions for determining freight rates, and usually no procedures for prior consultation. The time of notice is not necessarily specified.

(b) Specific freight rates

There are procedures for determining freight rates on new cargo items and handling requests from shippers for reductions of specific freight rates, but no procedures for consultation on increases of specific freight rates.

(c) Promotional freight rates

There are usually no specific provisions for determining promotional freight rates.

(continued)

35

TABLE 3.1 (continued)

Feature	Comment
(d) Surcharges	Surcharges are imposed without prior notice and often without specific justification.
(e) Currencies—devaluation, revaluation, rates of exchange, floating currencies	Procedures for consultation existing in Western Europe in connection with devaluation or revaluation of tariff currencies do not seem to operate effectively. There are no procedures regarding floating currencies.
Other matters	
(a) Outside competition	There are devices to prevent or eliminate outside competition.
(b) Averaging of freight rates	There is provision for the averaging of freight rates over port ranges.
(c) Quality of service	There is usually no provision regarding the type or other characteristics of the shipping to be used.
(d) Adequacy of service	The responsibility for providing adequate service usually rests with individual lines.

Source: UNCTAD, The Regulation of Liner Conferences (TD/104/Rev. 1) (New York: United Nations, 1972).

construction differences exist in that liners are usually able to generate higher speeds, and their holds are often compartmentalized for carrying finished or semifinished manufactures, or even such "sensitive" goods as butter, sugar, coffee, or cocoa.* However, liners and tramps are similar enough that the latter can be brought into service on liner routes for short periods of time.

Perhaps the best way of distinguishing between tramps and liners is to note the types of cargoes generally handled by each. For example, Table 3.2 provides one set of estimates of the relative importance of different categories of goods in total tramp ship charterings. Grains and seeds comprise over 50 percent of loadings, and the proportion rises to about 75 percent if ores, coal, and coke are also included. Another noteworthy point is that the general cargo category, which constitutes a high proportion of liner conference loadings, represents only about 1 percent of tramp cargoes.[2]

In contrast to Table 3.2, liner cargoes are generally materials or goods that do not lend themselves to shipment either by tramp vessels or by industrially owned fleets. As such, "normal" liner conference cargoes are usually manufactured goods or materials such as tea, rubber, or jute that have been partly processed and are packaged before shipment. However, in some cases liners will seek out certain bulk cargoes such as coal, ores, or metal scrap for bottom stowage.

In spite of the physical similarities between liners and tramps, and the fact that they may transport similar cargoes on occasion, important institutional differences exist in the markets each serves. Liners operate within the conference framework that regulates entry of new members and the types of competition involved. In contrast, tramps and other bulk carriers normally operate in markets that are more competitive and responsive to supply and demand changes. To a large degree, this is because the tramp market is not encumbered

---

*Within the liner group a distinction is often made between the "break bulk" ship and the container ship. A break bulk ship is designed to carry a heterogeneous cargo, each consignment being separately packed without any uniform style or pattern. Efficient space utilization, however, requires long periods in port loading cargo. In contrast, container ships utilize standard unitized packaging devices that allow much of the loading to be done in the absence of the mother ship itself. Once the vessel arrives in port, the fully loaded containers can be quickly loaded through the use of specialized cranes and handling devices.

TABLE 3.2

Principal Cargoes Carried by Tramp Shipping Services
over the Period 1964-67

Nature of Cargo Carried	Percentage (by weight) of Total			
	1964	1965	1966	1967
Grains and seeds	54.23	60.08	58.45	53.45
Ferrous and nonferrous ores	12.88	10.03	11.14	11.29
Coal and coke	11.54	10.55	7.39	10.00
Metals/scrap	5.84	3.74	5.34	6.26
Fertilizers and salt	2.33	2.78	4.14	5.40
Phosphate rock	3.25	3.13	3.11	4.05
Sugar	4.00	4.16	4.09	3.61
Sulfur	1.65	1.78	2.20	2.76
Unspecified general cargo	0.84	1.20	1.50	0.94
Timber/wood products	1.77	0.99	1.16	0.94
Copra	0.58	0.78	0.77	0.66
Cement	0.84	0.42	0.50	0.46
Pyrites	0.18	0.15	0.11	0.15
Esparto	0.07	0.21	0.10	0.03

Source: UNCTAD, Level and Structure of Freight Rates, Conference Practices and Adequacy of Shipping Services (New York: United Nations, 1969).

by the various competitive restraining features associated with the liner system. The fact that the tramp market is more competitive is one reason why it has not been subject to the criticism directed at liners. However, many developing countries are not able to utilize tramp services since this involves chartering a whole ship for a given run. Developing countries often cannot generate the size of consignments necessary to make tramp chartering economically feasible, apart from the limitations imposed by the liner conferences (such as deferred rebates and loyalty contracts) on their ability to do so.

Given the differences in competitive conditions and markets, questions have been raised about the relation between liner and tramp rates. In this respect, it is acknowledged that liner rates are more stable than those for tramps. However, this should be expected since stability is a characteristic of administered prices. Since liners and tramps may compete for some similar goods, attempts have also been made to draw inferences between their respective freight rates. A point that must be noted, however, is that comparisons between the level or trend of liner and tramp rates are not valid because each basically refers to a different type of service. For example, the liner rate normally includes cargo handling charges while the tramp rate usually does not. The tramp rate is a whole ship rate whereas liner charges are for parcels. The liner provides regular service ready for use when a shipper wants it, and need not be used when nothing is available for transport. In contrast, tramps provide a service for a shipper who can fill a vessel. For similar reasons, comparisons of liner and tramp rates in relation to the value of the product carried are not valid.

THE MARKET FOR BULK CARRIERS AND TANKERS

Two types of specialized shipping services also have an important influence on developing country trade. The first is bulk carriers: specialized ships designed to transport crude materials such as ores over long distances; the second involves tankers that transport petroleum, other liquid cargoes, and even grains. While it is generally held that the markets for these carrier services are governed largely by changes in supply and demand, there is some basis for suggesting that oligopolistic elements have the potential to influence rate setting. Specifically, a substantial portion of these vessels, especially tankers, comprises merchant fleets owned or controlled by oil or vertically integrated mining companies. Interlocking directorates may also result in preferential chartering of carriers owned by established shipping lines of developed countries, as in the case of steel mills that are closely associated with shipping lines of bulk carrier fleets. Developed countries, which are generally major importers of crude materials, normally purchase products shipped in bulk carriers on an f.o.b. basis and are in a better position to select the ship to be chartered. This could give some leverage in the bargaining for bulk carrier services.

However, a major factor that has kept monopoly elements from having an important influence on price formation has been the substantial overcapacity in world tanker markets that persisted throughout most of the 1970s. As an illustration, Table 3.3 provides estimates

TABLE 3.3

Estimated Productivity of Tankers, Tons Carried, and Ton-Miles Logged
Per Deadweight Ton in 1970 and 1973–79

Year	Total Shipments of Oil and Grain in Tankers (million tons)	Total Shipments of Oil and Grain in Tankers* (thousand million ton-miles)	Total Tanker Fleet (million dwt)	Tons of Cargo Carried Per dwt	Ton-Miles Per dwt (thousand)
1970	1,182	6,039	137.8	8.58	43.82
1973	1,479	8,915	198.2	7.46	45.00
1974	1,491	9,543	230.5	6.47	41.40
1975	1,386	8,922	272.9	5.08	32.69
1976	1,563	10,335	306.6	5.10	33.71
1977	1,591	10,527	327.3	4.86	32.16
1978	1,589	9,982	329.9	4.82	30.26
1979	1,654	10,232	327.6	5.05	31.23

*Expressed in terms of the tonnage shipped times the distance covered by the shipment.

Source: UNCTAD, Review of Maritime Transport, 1979 (TD/B/C.4/198) (Geneva: United Nations, 1980).

of the productivity of the world tanker fleet in terms of tons carried and ton-miles per existing deadweight ton (dwt) over the period 1970-79. These figures show the magnitude of existing overcapacity as the carriage figure per dwt in 1979 had fallen to about 60 percent of that for the beginning of the decade. Productivity figures for bulk carriers also show evidence of persistent overcapacity, but probably not to the same extent as for tankers. For example, in 1970, 8.4 tons were carried per dwt of bulk carrier while in 1979 the figure was 5.8 tons (a drop of 30 percent). Similarly, the ton-miles per dwt of bulk carriers fell from 39,400 in 1970 to 29,100 in 1979.

If developing countries attempt to move into the bulk carrier or tanker trade, a problem that will undoubtedly pose an important constraint concerns the fact that steady increases in size, technical sophistication, and construction costs involve increasingly greater capital expenditures. The magnitude of the investment now required could be a factor leading to greater pressure for regulation of competition through adoption of some features of the liner conference system.* This would be a negative development from the developing countries' viewpoint given their antagonism to the conferences. However, a potentially important competitive stimulus is that the OPEC countries are showing a growing interest in expanding operations into the carriage of the petroleum products they produce.

THE RELATIVE IMPORTANCE OF SHIPPING SERVICES

A key point to emerge from the preceding discussion was that important differences exist between the markets in which developing countries purchase required shipping services. Tramp, bulk carrier, and tanker operations are generally contracted in much more competitive markets than those for liners. Thus, any assessment of developing country shipping problems must consider the relative volume of exports and imports transported by these different types of vessels. Given the moderating influence of competition on prices, profits, and performance, a different view of the importance of

---

*As an illustration, UNCTAD estimates that the construction cost of a 30,000-dwt product tanker rose from $10 million to $23 million over 1970-79, and the cost of the same size bulk carrier increased from $8.7 million to $15.5 million. However, for larger vessels such as a 400,000-dwt tanker the 1979 construction cost was put at $60 million.[3]

developing country shipping problems would emerge if a high proportion of their trade is carried in tramps or bulk carriers as opposed to the liner conferences.

Unfortunately, available evidence indicates that the conferences are of primary importance in the trade of many developing countries. For example, P. J. Richards notes that

> conferences carry a very large percentage of the general cargo (that is, total trade less fuels less crude materials) exports of developing countries. In the India-UK/Continental trade and in the India-US trade probably some 80 to 90 percent of general cargo is handled by the conferences; 95 percent of Argentina's general cargo exports are also carried by the conferences. Eighty percent of Senegal's general cargo exports to France, 99 percent of the Cameroons' exports to the UK/Continent, and 80 percent of her exports to the US are taken by conferences.[4]

In a detailed empirical analysis, Karl Fashbender and Wolfgang Wagner also conclude that liner conferences are of paramount importance in the export and import trade of most developing countries. While it was noted that tankers handle the primary share of petroleum exporting countries' outward trade, and bulk carriers are of major importance in the trade of countries like Bolivia, Mauritania, Surinam, Ecuador, and Cuba that export crude materials (tin, iron ore, bauxite, bananas, and sugar, respectively), persuasive evidence is developed by these authors that shows liners play a key role in the export trade of other nations, particularly those that rely more heavily on exports of manufactures.[5] For example, it is estimated that liners handle between one-half and two-thirds of the entire seaborne trade of India and about three-quarters of Brazil's total maritime trade. These and other examples provide evidence that the liner conferences are a primary factor in the export trade of developing countries that have made the transition to semiprocessed and manufactured exports. However, even for those countries that primarily are exporters of bulk materials or petroleum, Fashbender and Wagner conclude that "on the import side, the liner trade is essential for all developing countries since their imports overwhelmingly consist of manufactured products which reach them as general (liner) cargo."[6] This finding accents the fact that for most developing countries liners have a key position in the export trade, and have a dominant position in the carriage of imports.

DISCRIMINATION AND LINER CONFERENCES

The analysis of market characteristics, and evaluation of the relative importance of different types of shipping services, shows why developing countries are so concerned with the functioning of the liner conference system. In addition to the anticompetitive practices of the conferences, perhaps the most inflammatory complaints against these associations involve charges of discrimination. To some degree these charges are based on the presumption that conference lines, normally headquartered in developed nations, deliberately favor their own countries' exports, or the exports of other industrial nations. Similarly, accusations have also included charges that shipping conferences deliberately discriminate in favor of given ports or routes, against incoming as opposed to outgoing trade, against specific types of products, or against small versus large shippers.

As a general proposition, discrimination in ocean freight rates or services is held to exist when the liner charge for a particular product contributes more (or less) to the costs and profits required to provide for its shipment than can be explained by some objective method of allocating costs and profits.* The economic basis for discrimination is that some exporters have fewer transport alternatives or ship products that are less sensitive to freight charges than others. In economic terms, such exporters have a relatively inelastic demand for transport services and can be made to bear a freight rate higher than is justified by cost considerations alone. Other shippers who have more options for transport, or export products that are more sensitive to freight charges, have a relatively elastic demand for transport. In such cases, it may be profitable to apply somewhat lower freight rates than justified by pure cost considerations.

It must be noted, however, that freight rate discrimination need not be intentional. For example, UNCTAD acknowledges that

---

*Fashbender and Wagner adopt a similar line in noting that transport price differentials are justified only by differences in the actual cost-of-carriage. If freight rate differences cannot be explained by corresponding cost differentials they are objectively unjustified and should be classified as rate discrimination. The discrimination argument, therefore, hinges on whether freight rate differences can be justified on the basis of cost of operations.

random or accidental discrimination by liner companies can arise from a reluctance to revise freight rate schedules. Trading patterns and market forces change constantly with the result that liner conferences rate policy may lag behind current developments. As such, an existing freight structure may appear discriminatory because it reflects conditions that prevailed in the past. Besides possible rate distortions due to such factors, shipping conferences are continually faced with the problem of rate setting for a wide variety of products traded among the ports and countries they service. Often liners attempt to resolve this rate-setting problem by classifying commodities in broad groups and pricing their shipment by range. This administrative procedure may result in some commodities being discriminated against because of an imperfect pricing mechanism. However, whether accidental or intentional, the existence of such discriminatory freight rates can have important economic consequences for developing country exporters.

Discrimination between Countries

While many developing countries have expressed similar charges, discriminatory freight rates have also been a topic of concern to the United States, and information produced by this nation is useful for illustrating the nature of the problem. Specifically, in the early 1960s, ocean freight rate hearings were conducted by the U.S. Congress Joint Economic Committee under the chairmanship of Senator Douglass. According to the Douglass Committee, ocean freight rates from the United States to Europe and other parts of the world were found to be higher than those for similar products shipped to the United States.* Moreover, freight rates from the United States to nearby destinations were often found to be higher than comparable charges from Europe over much longer hauls. As such, the Douglass Committee report concluded that "the international ocean freight

---

*For example, the report showed it cost $38.25 to ship a long ton of steel tubing from New York to the German Federal Republic. In contrast, the German exporter paid for shipping a slightly lighter metric ton to the United States no more than $20.75. Data produced by the Douglass Committee also showed that the export rates for U.S. steel products to Japan, France, and the German Federal Republic were on arithmetic average 60 percent higher than the corresponding import rates.[7]

structure is weighted against United States exports. Our exports
bear most of the cost of vessel operation, even in trades where imports approximate exports in value and quantity."[8]

In finding number 3, the Douglass Committee concluded that
liner companies acting in concert can practice national discrimination
through the structure of the charges they adopt. The report specifically noted that

> most ocean freight rates are established by steamship
> conferences whose basic purpose is to set freight rates
> and sailing schedules. But some go beyond price fixing
> and include pooling arrangements whereby each member
> is guaranteed a share of cargo or revenues. United States
> flag lines are outnumbered in all but 7 of the more than
> 100 active steamship conferences involved in United States
> foreign trade. In substance, foreign lines, some of which
> are government owned, determine freight rates, sailing
> schedules and other conditions vital to the expansion of
> American commerce.[9]

The Joint Economic Committee thus concluded it was possible for a
group of liner companies, acting as a conference, to set rates and
operating conditions that discriminate between the nations they service. Related complaints have suggested that due to their oligopolistic market position the conferences have achieved unduly high profits
on freight carried between developed and developing countries; profits
that influence the export performance and industrialization prospects
of the latter.

Some indication as to the basis for these charges of national
discrimination can be had from Table 3.4. The table shows freight
rates and nautical mileage associated with the transport of similar
products shipped from two different developing countries to the Federal Republic of Germany. At first glance, the data seemingly show
evidence of national discrimination. For example, shipments of
beef from Brazil bear higher freight rates than similar shipments
from Argentina, even though the latter is almost 1,000 nautical miles
further from the German ports. Similar rate distance reversals
also occur for cocoa, timber, tea, jute, and rice.

In a detailed analysis of these freight rate differences, Fashbender and Wagner conclude that they can be largely accounted for
by such factors as the quality of vessels employed on the liner runs,
the extent to which these vessels are fully utilized, differences in
port time or loading costs, differences in volume shipped, duration
of run, or the degree of competition (from tramps) and countervailing
power on the part of shippers. As such, what appears to be evidence

TABLE 3.4

Net Freight Rates Prevailing for Selected Products and Ports to the Antwerp–Hamburg Area
(rates in terms of dollars or marks)

Product/Unit/Exporter	Port of Export	Net Rate in U.S. or DM	Distance to Hamburg (nautical miles)	Net Rate Per 100 Nautical Miles
Concentrated juices (1,000 kg)				
Greece	Salonica	69.93 DM	3,360	2.08 DM
Israel	Haifa	100.00 DM	3,694	2.71 DM
Cotton (1,000 kg)				
United States	New Orleans	60.63 $	5,225	1.16 $
United Arab Republic	Alexandria	26.87 $	3,444	0.78 $
Raw tobacco (1,000 kg)				
Brazil	Salvador	274.55 DM	4,837	4.89 DM
Greece	Porto Alegre	155.50 DM	3,360	4.63 DM
Coffee (1,000 kg)				
Brazil	Santos	54.03 $	5,705	0.95 $
Guatemala	Santo Tomas	47.60 $	5,295	0.91 $
Frozen beef boneless (1,000 kg)				
Argentina	Buenos Aires	153.00 DM	6,619	2.31 DM
Brazil	Santos	160.00 DM	5,705	2.80 DM

Frozen beef bone in (1,000 kg)				
Argentina	Buenos Aires	170.00 DM	6,619	2.57 DM
Brazil	Santos	180.00 DM	5,705	3.16 DM
Cocoa (1,000 kg)				
Dominican Republic	Santo Domingo	50.67 $	4,340	1.17 $
Ecuador	Guayaquil	53.10 $	5,940	0.89 $
Sawn timber (cubic board meters)				
Ivory Coast	Abidjan	27.86 $	3,983	0.70 $
Tanzania	Dar-es-Salaam	24.93 $	8.773	0.28 $
Tea (40 cubic feet)				
Ceylon	Colombo	31.41 $	10,937	0.29 $
India	Calcutta	29.06 $	12,187	0.24 $
Jute (40 cubic feet)				
East-Pakistan	Chittagong	25.75 $	12,187	0.21 $
Thailand	Bangkok	23.22 $	12,891	0.18 $
Rice (40 cubic feet)				
Thailand	Bangkok	31.31 $	12,891	0.24 $
Peoples Republic of China	Shanghai	19.89 $	14,274	0.14 $

Source: Karl Fashbender and Wolfgang Wagner, Shipping Conferences, Rate Policy and Developing Countries (Hamburg: Verlag Weltarchiv, 1973), p. 112. Reprinted by permission from the author and the publisher.

of national discrimination often can be accounted for by variations in underlying market factors. This conclusion, that cost-related considerations often are reflected in national rate differences, seems to have been generally accepted by transport economists who have investigated such questions.

Discrimination against Products

Aside from the level of conference charges, freight rate structure has been subject to frequent criticism by developing countries. Allegations have been made that conference rates favor the export of primary goods at the expense of semifinished products or manufactures. It is further held that such discrimination can have serious detrimental effects on export prices and revenues. For example, an UNCTAD analysis noted that an ocean freight rate that resulted in even a 2 percent export price disadvantage might inhibit growth of the producing industry and have an important retardation effect on the scale of production that could increase over time.[10]

Table 3.5 provides an example of the type of documentation employed, in this case by the government of India, to illustrate alleged freight rate discrimination against products. Shown here are freight rates for selected commodities shipped from India to Port Said and the United Kingdom to Port Said. In assessing this information, it should be noted that the nautical distance between major Indian ports and Port Said is about 90 percent of that from the United Kingdom. Thus, prima facie evidence suggests that Indian freight rates should be lower if distance is a factor influencing transport charges. However, it can be seen that the U.K. freight rates vary between 29.2 and 98 percent of those for India, with half being between 83.7 and 91.2 percent. If this sample of products is representative, the data suggest that ratios below 80 percent, such as those for dry chilies, coir fibers, mats, and yarns, discriminate against Indian exporters of these products.

Since the evidence concerning freight rate product discrimination has an important bearing on developing country industrialization objectives, it will be examined in more detail in Chapter 5. However, it should be noted at this point that several different sources of information do provide substantial evidence of product discrimination by the conferences, especially between primary and processed goods.

Discrimination against Shippers

Earlier in this chapter it was shown that liner conferences have several ways of differentiating between individual shippers. For

TABLE 3.5

Comparison of Ocean Freight Rates for Common Shipments
from India and the United Kingdom to Port Said

| Commodity | Freight Rate to Port Said | | | Ratio of U.K. to Indian Rate |
	Indian	U.K.	Basis	
Rayon piece goods	182 6d	166s 6d	cubic meter	91.2
Rayon yarn	182s 6d	166s 6d	cubic meter	91.2
Dry chilies	550s	330s 9d	1,000 kilos	60.1
Coir fiber	280s	166s 6d	1,000 kilos	59.5
Coir mats	570s	166s 6d	1,000 kilos	29.2
Coir yarn[a]	305s	257s	1,000 kilos	84.3
Coir yarn[b]	455s	257s	1,000 kilos	56.5
Cotton piecegoods	182s 6d	166s 6d	cubic meter	91.2
Cotton thread	182s 6d	166s 6d	cubic meter	91.2
Cotton fabrics	180s	149s 6d	cubic meter	83.1
Kapok	132s 6d	107s 9d	cubic meter	81.3
Lac, shell	392s 6d	330s 9d	1,000 kilos	84.3
Lemon grass oil	485s	330s 9d	1,000 kilos	68.2
Cigarette paper	152s 6d	149s 6d	cubic meter	98.0
Plastic manufactures	225s	183s 9d	cubic meter	81.7
Canned shrimp	150s	135s	cubic meter	90.0
Leather shoes	182s 6d	149s 6d	cubic meter	81.9
Sporting goods	192s 6d	166s 6d	1,000 kilos	89.6
Tires and tubes	182s 6d	149s 6d	1,000 kilos	81.9
Unenumerated cargo	235s	210s	1,000 kilos	87.2
Wooden articles	180s	149s 6d	1,000 kilos	81.9
Woolen piecegoods	182s 6d	149s 6d	cubic meter	81.9

[a] Hydraulically pressed.
[b] Hand pressed.

Source: Adapted from UNCTAD, Level and Structure of Freight Rates, Conference Practices and the Adequacy of Shipping Services (New York: United Nations, 1969), p. 92.

example, shippers can be coerced into signing loyalty contracts that tie them to the liner conferences. Exporters who do not enter into such agreements are subject to higher freight rates and other less favorable terms of service. Thus a common contractual procedure followed by the conferences unquestionably results in rate differences between individual shippers.

Another developing country complaint is that conferences discriminate on the basis of consignment size, with smaller shippers bearing higher freight rates. Liner conference freight schedules often list quantity discounts depending on the size of shipment, while larger exporters may utilize their bargaining power to secure secret concessions. However, arguments that such rate differentials constitute discrimination must face the problem of how to show that loyalty contracts, which result in rate differentials for individual shippers, or consignment size, are not related to actual differences in the cost-of-carriage since the conferences argue that both institutional factors contribute to lower operating expenses. For example, loyalty contracts are linked to rationalized planning of transport services since shipment frequencies and sizes are better known. Size and quantity discounts have also been justified by the conferences on the basis of scale economies that purportedly result in lower unit operating costs. However, considerable debate surrounds the importance of such factors with the result that questions concerning discrimination between shippers remain essentially open.

Before turning from the discussion of discrimination, one point should be made concerning the controversy surrounding this issue. Whether the allegations involve discrimination between countries, products, or shippers, the charge always rests on the proposition that actual freight rates do not reflect the true cost-of-carriage. As such, the liner conferences could do much to combat such charges, if unsubstantiated, by making operating cost data available for analysis. However, the conferences have persistently followed a very protective and secretive policy with regard to such information. This policy has undoubtedly contributed to the general feeling that the conferences have something to hide and that rate discrimination is in fact practiced.

PORT DEVELOPMENT AND LINER CONFERENCES

Before turning from the topic, it should be noted that there is an additional developing country transport problem connected with liner conference pricing procedures. Specifically, the conference practice of averaging freight rates over ports of call is an important element in developing country port development problems. This rate-setting procedure results in an important disincentive to port improvements since savings will be distributed over all stops on the liner route. Thus, only where a liner is limited to two ports might innovators realize full benefits from their investment. If several ports are included on a liner route the gains will be dissipated; the larger the number of ports, the smaller the share of benefits accruing to the one making the improvement. However, an even more pessimistic view suggests that benefits from port investments are normally absorbed by liners as higher profits with no corresponding reductions in freight rates. The resulting uncertainty as to whether benefits will be averaged or absorbed by the conferences has been a serious disincentive to make port improvements.*

A related assessment of port problems concluded that escalating port operation costs are causing major problems for developing countries since they are unable to absorb these charges.[11] Specifically, this UNCTAD study examined the increase in port costs originating from the following elements:

Port charges

Charges for services to vessels (for pilotage, towage, berth occupancy, and so on)

Cargo-handling charges

Wharf-handling charges (that is, charges for handling up to the ship's hook in a loading port, and from the ship's hook in a loading port, and from a ship's hook onward in a discharging port)

Stevedoring charges (that is, charges for taking on board and stowing in a loading port, and unloading and landing on the wharf in a discharging port)

———————————————

*As a partial solution, UNCTAD proposes that free-in-and-out (f.i.o.) rate-making systems be adopted. Such a procedure would allow separate identification of transport versus port costs, with the result that the relation between the latter and any port improvements could be directly examined. It appears that such a procedure might also discourage the averaging of freight rates over several ports of call since the freight cost elements on each stage of the liner run would be more visible. It should be noted that transport charges in the bulk trade are normally stated independent of port charges, so such a disincentive to port modernization does not exist for such shipments.

Costs of ship's time involved (normal charges associated with idle
port time while the vessel is being loaded or unloaded)*

The finding that emerged was that rapidly rising developed-country
stevedoring charges were a major factor behind the overall increase
in port costs, and they were having a serious retardation effect on
developing country trade. An earlier but related analysis by L. M. S.
Rajwar also found that stevedoring costs were having serious adverse
effects on developing country exports. Specifically, this study noted
that

> The effect of rising stevedoring costs is perhaps the
> most difficult, and thus far, intractable problem facing
> the shipping and trade of developing countries. Although
> these countries are in no way responsible for rising la-
> bor costs in developed countries, their economies ulti-
> mately bear the burden of these costs. In some cases,
> the developing countries have tried to counterbalance the
> effect of higher stevedoring costs by increasing direct
> or indirect export incentives. But this process cannot
> be continued beyond a certain point without causing seri-
> ous distortions in the economies of exporting countries.
> The export potential of developing countries, particularly
> for primary commodities, may be seriously affected un-
> less some method can be evolved to protect the trade of
> developing countries from the impact of increased steve-
> doring costs in the ports of developed countries.[12]

However, while this problem has been acknowledged in a number of
investigations, no effective proposals have yet been made for offsetting
rising stevedoring costs.

------

*In liner shipping the costs of ship's time, vessel charges,
and charges for stevedoring are all borne by the shipowner and covered by the freight rates. Liner operators recover increases in
these costs by periodically raising the level of their freight rates.
However, under voyage charter or contract (that is, tramp) arrangements the shipowner agrees to bear only the "normal" amount of
ship's time for cargo handling operations. If the charter takes longer
than a stipulated period to load or discharge the vessel, then he normally must pay demurrage to the shipowner.

THE FLAGS OF CONVENIENCE ISSUE

A further institutional problem facing developing countries concerns flags of convenience. Stated simply, flags of convenience comprise all vessels that are registered in countries with which they have no genuine economic link. This implies that the flag state has no share in a vessel's beneficial ownership, and does not provide a major part of its crew. Statistics now suggest that these flags of convenience vessels comprise about 30 percent of the world fleet. Table 3.6 provides a breakdown of the true ownership of these open-registry vessels.

In a recent study, UNCTAD examined the repercussions of phasing out this system of ship registration.[13] This report argues that the main beneficiaries of such a move would be the developing countries, since five developed countries accounting for 81 percent of the beneficial ownership fleet (the United States, Greece, Hong Kong, Japan, and the Federal Republic of Germany) probably could not repatriate such ships because of high labor costs or a shortage of skilled seamen. The developing countries could offer an adequate supply of shipboard labor at low cost and would therefore get an opportunity to carry more of the large volume of world tonnage now handled by these vessels.

UNCTAD's analysis of the economic consequences of a phase out on the host countries (that is, the countries that operate open registries) shows that the benefits from these operations may be smaller than generally assumed. Specifically, the gains through operating such registers even for the major open-registry country (Liberia) do not amount to more than 3 percent of its gross national product. Furthermore, UNCTAD sees the positive aspect of phasing out open registries as giving developing countries an opportunity to develop as real shipowners, ending "their present, degrading role as nominal shipowners." Since open-registry countries receive none of the profits made by their flags of convenience, and employment of their nationals is minimal, a relatively small increase in real ownership would outweigh revenue losses associated with the phasing out of vessels they only nominally own.

One of the main effects of establishing a genuine link between vessels and the flag they fly would be to bring employment of seafarers within the jurisdiction of the country of registration. This would have a beneficial influence upon conditions of employment since, in the case of open-registry vessels, jurisdiction is exercised neither by the country of the nominal flag, nor by the country of the beneficial owners, nor by the country of the crew members. In this situation, working conditions are governed by

TABLE 3.6

Beneficial Ownership of Open-Registry Vessels in 1978
(number of vessels and thousand deadweight tons)

Countries of Beneficial Owners*	Liberia		Panama		Singapore		Cyprus		Bermuda		Hong Kong		Bahamas		Total	
	Number	Thousand dwt	Number	Thousand dwt	Number	Thousand dwt	Number	Thousand dwt	Number	Thousand dwt	Number	Thousand dwt	Number	Thousand dwt	Number	Thousand dwt
United States	576	55,647	213	6,212	2	6	2	8	11	425	—	—	11	77	815	62,375
Greece	571	35,482	141	1,516	17	405	475	3,047	4	216	—	—	—	—	1,208	40,666
Hong Kong	550	27,261	283	5,650	28	179	2	2	—	—	13	212	—	—	876	33,304
Japan	168	7,394	421	5,361	75	5,349	—	—	—	—	—	—	—	—	664	18,104
Germany, Fed. Rep. of	72	2,911	54	582	145	1,739	52	201	3	28	—	—	—	—	326	5,461
Unspecified	56	1,553	180	1,949	3	20	6	55	—	—	—	—	—	—	239	3,522
Italy	37	2,642	52	417	—	—	1	19	1	81	—	—	—	—	96	3,195
Switzerland	84	2,477	53	516	3	77	—	—	—	—	2	72	—	—	141	3,089
Singapore	5	141	53	193	297	2,334	—	—	—	—	—	—	—	—	357	2,740
Canada	14	402	4	21	—	—	—	—	47	2,198	1	57	2	20	68	2,698
Israel	37	1,969	7	350	9	204	8	44	—	—	—	—	—	—	53	2,523
United Kingdom	53	1,796	15	98	31	47	7	13	5	86	9	213	—	—	121	2,284
Norway	38	1,737	9	90	12	87	2	18	4	49	1	35	—	—	71	2,011
Netherlands	30	935	46	248	—	—	—	—	—	—	—	—	—	—	78	1,201
Monaco	23	855	2	72	—	—	—	—	2	126	—	—	—	—	27	1,053
Korea, Dem. People's Rep. of	14	283	80	709	1	57	—	—	—	—	—	—	—	—	95	1,049
Countries and entities each beneficially owning less than 1 million dwt	155	4,536	281	2,837	26	284	15	61	4	44	7	134	14	96	502	7,992
Unidentified	60	2,415	269	824	—	—	140	323	—	—	—	—	—	—	469	3,562
World	2,543	150,436	2,163	27,645	649	10,788	710	3,791	81	3,253	33	723	27	193	6,206	196,829
Share in total open-registry fleets	41.0	76.4	34.9	14.0	10.5	5.5	11.4	1.9	1.3	1.7	0.5	0.4	0.4	0.1	100.0	100.0

Countries of Registration

*Beneficial owner is the person, company, or organization that gains the pecuniary benefits from the shipping operations.

Source: UNCTAD, Handbook of International Trade Statistics (New York: United Nations, 1979), p. 658.

shipowners or their managing agents, and by conditions enforced by seafaring unions.

A major finding of the UNCTAD report on open registries contradicts assumptions that freight costs would rise if there were a phasing out of these operations. The freight rate increase argument is normally based on the assertion that shipping tonnage now carried in flags of convenience vessels would have to shift to high-cost developed country carriers. However, the phasing out of open registries would probably provide an important stimulus to the development of developing country national fleets. Lower national wages and other operating factors suggest that transport charges in developing country vessels might even be lower than those for open-registry carriers.

NOTES

1. M. G. Valente, "The Participation of Developing Countries in Shipping," in Shipping and Developing Countries (New York: Carnegie Endowment, 1971), p. 37.

2. For an excellent description of the characteristics and economics of tramp shipping markets, see B. N. Metaxes, The Economics of Tramp Shipping (London: Athlone Press, 1971).

3. See UNCTAD, Review of Maritime Transport, 1979 (TD/B/C.4/198) (Geneva: United Nations, 1980).

4. P. J. Richards, "Shipping Problems of Underdeveloped Countries," Bulletin of the Oxford University Institute of Economics and Statistics 20 (August 1968):269.

5. Karl Fashbender and Wolfgang Wagner, Shipping Conferences, Rate Policy and Developing Countries (Hamburg: Verlag Weltarchiv, 1973).

6. Ibid., p. 80.

7. For a more detailed analysis of issues involved in this controversy concerning North American freight rates, see Esra Bennathan and A. A. Walters, The Economics of Ocean Freight Rates (New York: Praeger, 1972).

8. Discriminatory Ocean Freight Rates and the Balance of Payments. Hearings before the Joint Economic Committee, 88th Cong., 1st sess., January 1963-64, p. 374.

9. Ibid, p. 382.

10. UNCTAD, Level and Structure of Freight Rates, Conference Practices and Adequacy of Shipping Services (New York: United Nations, 1969).

11. UNCTAD, Causes of Increases in Port Costs and Their Impact (TD/B/C.4/167) (Geneva: United Nations, April 1977).

12. L. M. S. Rajar, "Trade and Shipping Needs of Developing Countries," in International Conciliation, Shipping and Developing Countries (New York: Carnegie Endowment, 1971), pp. 16-17.

13. UNCTAD, The Repercussions of Phasing Out Open Registries (TD/B/C.4/AC.1/5) (Geneva: United Nations, 1979).

4

TRANSPORT COSTS AND
DEVELOPING COUNTRY EXPORTS

Theoretical models of the development process often assign
a key role to various aspects of commercial trade policy. In such a
framework, export earnings are of prime importance to developing
countries since these revenues are used to purchase capital equipment and other goods required for industrialization and growth. However, economists are generally agreed that there are other benefits
from international trade that can have important long-term consequences. These include increasing returns connected with economies
of scale and market size, learning effects and the improvement of
human capital, beneficial results from competition and close communication with advanced countries, and potentially favorable demon-
stration effects.[1]

Aside from the theoretical arguments, recent empirical studies
also support the proposition that trade provides an important stimulus to growth and development. For example, Michael Michaely
correlated the rate of change in exports as a percentage of gross
national product (GNP) against that in per capita national product for
41 developing countries over the years 1950–73 and found a highly
significant positive relation between the variables.[2] The association
between economic growth and increases in the export share was particularly strong for the more advanced developing countries (Taiwan,
Israel, Korea, Yugoslavia, and so on), while the least developed
countries were generally characterized by stagnant export sectors
and low or negative growth rates.

In a related investigation, Benjamin Cohen employed a mul-
tiple regression model to assess the relative impact of additional
export earnings and additional foreign aid on developing countries'
GNP.[3] In each of the two time periods tested, the export variable's
regression coefficient was significant and considerably larger than
that for the foreign aid term. This was interpreted to mean that the
growth effects of additional export earnings are larger than those for
foreign aid. As an explanation, Cohen cites the contribution of the

dynamic productivity and learning effects of trade on growth, while foreign aid conveys relatively static benefits in these areas.

Robert Emery has also employed regression analysis to test the relation between export expansion and economic growth for a selection of 50 developed and developing countries.[4] As in the other studies, a high positive correlation between growth in exports and GNP was observed. This led Emery to conclude that, on average, a 2.5 percent increase in exports leads to a 1 percent increase in GNP, although there is considerable variation among individual countries.

Perhaps the most comprehensive analysis of the relation between trade and growth is the study by Irving Kravis.[5] A primary objective of this investigation was to test the hypothesis that the tremendous expansion of Western Europe's demand for foodstuffs and raw materials in the nineteenth century provided the basic inducement for the development of the periphery countries (that is, Canada, the United States, Australia, Argentina), and that trade in this period was an "engine of growth." The issue has important implications for current development policy. If demand conditions were basically different, the nineteenth-century model of growth through trade may be of little relevance to developing countries today.

The major conclusions of the study may be summarized as follows:

- Trade expansion should be seen as a "handmaiden" of successful growth rather than an autonomous engine of growth.
- Where growth occurred in the nineteenth century it was mainly the result of favorable internal factors.
- Export growth and increases in national product are correlated for developing countries today.
- External markets for developing countries are now more favorable than nineteenth-century markets were for the periphery countries.

The last finding is important since it implies that the size of current export markets is sufficient to support developing country development objectives. Specifically, Kravis concluded that

it is clear that the markets of today's center countries loom much larger relative to the output of the LDCs [less developed countries] than was the case in the nineteenth century. Also, post-Second World War markets have expanded about twice as fast per annum as in the nineteenth century, with the increase between 1950 and 1965 being more than four times the 1950 aggregate GDP [Gross Domestic Product] of the developing countries.[6]

TRANSPORT COSTS, TRADE, AND DEVELOPMENT

Given the theoretical and empirical evidence that ties export
expansion to economic growth and development, an important question concerns the magnitude of the barrier posed by transport costs
to developing country trade. In this respect, it must be noted that
the effects of freight costs are very similar to those of tariffs.
Shipping costs, like import duties, raise the landed price of foreign-
produced goods and thereby reduce the level of demand for these
items. A question of importance, therefore, concerns the magnitude
of these charges relative to such artificial trade control measures as
tariffs.

A study of transport costs for U.S. imports from <u>all sources</u>
accents the importance of freight rates as international trade barriers. Specifically, J. M. Finger and A. J. Yeats drew on a 1965
Census Bureau-Tariff Commission sample of approximately 13,000
shipments to the United States to estimate nominal and effective
rates of protection from tariffs and transportation costs.[7] Table 4.1
summarizes these results and also gives overall tariff and transport
averages using two different systems of weights; one based on all
OECD (Organization for Economic Cooperation and Development)
imports from other OECD countries, and the other on OECD imports
from developing countries.[*]

The data presented in Table 4.1 show that the overall degree
of protection afforded by international transportation costs is at
least as high as that from tariffs. Nominal transportation rates are
equal to or greater than tariffs for 25 of the 38 product groups, and
effective rates of transport protection as high as or higher than effective tariff rates for 20 of the groups. Overall, with both sets of

---

*The effective rates shown in Table 4.1 were estimated as
follows. If d_i and d_j are the nominal costs of transporting materials
and the final product, respectively, and t_i and t_j are the duties on
these items, then the effective rate of protection (E_j) from both
sources in a country that levies duties on f.o.b. values is

$$E_j = \frac{\Sigma(t_j + d_j) - \Sigma m(t_i + d_i)}{v} \tag{4.1}$$

where m is the material input coefficient and v the proportion of value added in free trade. It can be shown from the equation that the
effective rate of protection by tariffs and transport costs combined
is the sum of the effective rate of each source of protection.

TABLE 4.1

U.S. Nominal and Effective Rates of Protection from Post–Kennedy
Round Tariffs and Estimated Transport Costs

Commodity Group	Nominal Protection		Effective Protection		
	Tariffs	Transport	Tariffs	Transport	Total
Processed foods					
Meat products	6	6	10	15	25
Frozen fruits and vegetables	15	9	37	11	48
Preserved sea foods	6	10	16	10	26
Dehydrated foods	8	11	33	19	52
Pickles and dressings	9	13	−27	50	23
Roasted coffee	0	6	−2	4	2
Soft drinks	1	9	−10	12	2
Dairy products					
Cheese	12	8	35	14	49
Butter	10	8	47	21	68
Condensed milk	11	7	30	5	35

Grains and products

Corn milling	4	13	-2	21	19
Rice milling	37	17	328	106	434
Flour and cereal preparations	11	14	35	35	70
Prepared feeds	6	15	7	42	49
Bakery products	2	7	-4	4	0

Textiles and products

Wool yarn and thread	31	7	62	25	87
Wool fabrics	47	8	91	14	105
Wool clothing	27	8	7	9	16
Cotton yarn and thread	8	4	12	4	16
Cotton fabrics	16	6	31	20	51
Cotton clothing	20	8	34	8	42

Leather and products

Leather	6	4	19	4	23
Leather goods	4	10	4	18	22
Shoes	11	10	15	15	30

Lumber and paper products

Sawn wood	0	39	0	95	95
Plywood products	13	18	28	30	58
Wood manufactures	7	17	8	10	18
Wood pulp	0	12	-2	19	17
Paper and articles	5	13	13	10	23

(continued)

TABLE 4.1 (continued)

Commodity Group	Nominal Protection		Effective Protection		
	Tariffs	Transport	Tariffs	Transport	Total
Nonferrous metal products					
Nonmetallic mineral products	6	16	10	13	23
Glass and products	13	19	20	20	40
Nonferrous metals	6	5	14	5	19
Iron and steel					
Pig iron	1	15	6	24	30
Steel ingots	6	13	51	4	55
Metal manufactures	8	12	13	19	32
Machinery					
Nonelectric machines	7	7	9	8	17
Electrical machines	6	6	7	7	14
Agricultural machines	1	3	3	0	3
Average, weighted by OECD imports from					
Other OECD countries	8	9	13	14	27
Developing countries	8	10	15	17	32

Source: J. M. Finger and A. J. Yeats, "Effective Protection by Transportation Costs and Tariffs: A Comparison of Magnitudes," Quarterly Journal of Economics 90 (February 1976):171. Reprinted by permission.

weights the average nominal and effective rates of transport protection are slightly higher than their tariff counterparts, though within the accuracy of the figures it is reasonable to consider the tariff and transport cost averages as equal.

There are, of course, exceptions to this generalization. For each textile and for each dairy product group for which rates of protection were calculated, tariff protection, whether measured by nominal or effective rates, is considerably greater than that afforded by transportation costs. This, plus the extensive application of non-tariff import restrictions (which have not been accounted for in Table 4.1) in these industries, suggests strongly that transport costs are a minor part of total protection of these product lines. On the other hand, for those products of relatively high bulk and low unit values—lumber and paper products, for example—transport charges are a much larger part of the total protection enjoyed by these industries. While 6 of the 38 product groups have negative effective rates of tariff protection, none has negative rates of protection from transport costs, and the impact of transportation charges was more than sufficient to impart an overall positive effective rate for these items.

Table 4.1 also shows that the average effective rate exceeds the average nominal rate by the same amount for transport costs as for tariffs, whether imports from OECD countries or from developing countries are used as weights. This indicates that transportation costs, like tariffs, tend to escalate with stage of processing. Further, the average degree of escalation (measured by the effective rate minus the nominal rate) in both transportation costs and tariffs is slightly higher on U.S. imports from developing countries than on imports from developed countries.

Transport Profiles of Individual Countries

There are various reasons for believing that the transport cost data presented in Table 4.1 may understate the importance of freight costs for specific developing countries. First, the freight rates shown for each product group are averages for both developed and developing countries combined. Proximity to the U.S. market, size of shipment, or access to advanced shipping technology could all be factors leading to lower transport costs for developed countries. Second, to the extent that distance is a factor influencing freight rates, there might be large variations in transport costs for, say, Mexico as opposed to Thailand or Hong Kong.

For a more representative view of the importance of transport costs facing developing country exporters, information on these charges was compiled for India's exports to the United States.[8]

India was chosen as the exporting country because of its obvious importance among developing countries with a 1976 population of over 600 million people. Also, India exports a wide range of primary and manufactured goods to the North American market, so the potential exists for observing the incidence of transportation costs on a variety of products at different stages of fabrication. Finally, there is also reason to believe that the Indian transport cost profile should be representative of other important developing countries in South Asia.

Table 4.2 shows the average incidence of tariffs and transport costs on each three-digit SITC product that accounted for over $1 million in trade. Altogether, these 45 product groups had a combined value (f.a.s.) of over $500 million, or 85 percent of India's 1974 U.S. exports. To assist in evaluating these data, the table also shows the average transport factor on U.S. imports from all sources. Comparison of these figures with the transport rates for India shows the differential this country must pay as a result of its adverse location relative to some of its competitors. Finally, to assist in assessing the relative importance of transport and tariff costs on India's exports, both median and average values for these charges have been computed.

On an overall basis, the median transport rate for these 45 product groups (14.2 percent) is more than double that for the current level of U.S. MFN tariffs. Much the same picture concerning the relative importance of transport costs versus tariffs emerges from comparison of the average ad valorem incidence figures. For the product groups shown in Table 4.2, an average transport factor of 13.6 percent combines with an average tariff rate of 7.5 percent. When measured by averages, the spread between transport and tariff charges becomes 7.8 percent as opposed to a difference of 6.1 percent for the median figures.

A point that emerges from Table 4.2 is that considerable variation exists in the transport and tariff figures on an item-by-item basis. For example, woven textile products (SITC 653), India's largest single three-digit export product, experiences approximately equal (20 percent) transport and tariff barriers. It is also interesting to note that the existing transport differential between Indian exporters and their competitors (20.0 versus 5.8 percent) is one of the largest observed in the table. Much the same pattern exists for the other textile or related products, as India normally faces a transport cost differential of up to 18 percentage points (SITC 651). The fact that India is able to compete in the North American market in the face of such adverse transport costs may generally be attributed to the fact that its lower labor costs enable exporters to absorb this differential.

Aside from the incidence of transport costs on the textile and fabric products, the highest recorded ad valorem shipping rates appear for the metals and metal ores group. For example, ores of nonferrous base metals (SITC 283) have a transport factor of 52.8 percent, the highest recorded ad valorem rate for the 45 three-digit SITC items.* Furthermore, metal scrap, iron and steel castings, and iron and steel bars also register transport factors of 20 percent or more. Four other nontextile or nonmetal groups—footwear, wood manufactures, other crude materials, and leather—have rates in this range.

A key question centers on whether the results for India are typical, or if the transport cost profile for this nation is distorted by special considerations. To assess the reliability of the Indian tariff and transport averages, similar data were compiled for Indonesian exports to the United States. The results of these tabulations are summarized in Table 4.3.

On an overall average for the 40 product groups shown in the table, the transport rate is 11.8 percent, more than 5 percentage points higher than the average level of U.S. tariffs (6.4 percent) applied to these items. Much the same picture emerges from the figures excluding petroleum, although the spread between the two charges declines to 3.1 percentage points.

As was the case with India, there is considerable variation in the figures for individual products. The highest recorded ad valorem transport rate is 60.1 percent (SITC 899, manufactured articles), which is more than 45 percentage points above the corresponding tariff. Transport rates exceeding the corresponding tariffs by 30 points or more are also recorded for unworked and shaped wood, crude vegetable materials, printed matter, and food preparations. Conversely, for 9 of the 40 product groups, tariff charges exceed transport costs. Three of these groups (fixed vegetable oils, clothing, medicinal products including quinine) are of special importance to Indonesia with U.S. exports in excess of $1 million.

Table 4.3 shows that the ad valorem incidence of transport costs on Indonesian exports to the United States is not only higher than the average rate of U.S. tariffs, but also higher than the average rate of U.S. tariffs, but also higher than the average freight rate

---

*This exceptional figure is due to shipments of ilmenite sand, which has a transport factor of over 200 percent on shipments (c.i.f.) of approximately $800,000. India may not be making use of existing bulk shipping methods for this product, as a comparison with Australian figures shows the latter to have a transport factor for U.S. shipments that is more than 100 percentage points lower.

TABLE 4.2

Evaluation of the Ad Valorem Incidence of Most Favored Nation Tariffs and
International Transportation Costs on India's Exports to the United States

SITC	Description	Average Transport Rate for U.S. Imports	Rate for Indian Exports			1974 F.A.S. Value of Exports to the United States ($000)
			Transport Rate	Nominal Tariffs	Total	
653	Woven textile fabrics	5.8	20.0	19.4	39.4	136,090
652	Woven cotton fabrics	5.4	8.7	21.1	29.8	45,374
841	Clothing	8.0	15.9	22.1	38.0	39,354
667	Pearls and precious stones	0.5	0.8	2.5	3.3	36,495
051	Fresh fruit and nuts	12.7	6.4	6.4	12.8	34,659
061	Sugar and honey	6.8	9.3	4.3	13.6	32,512
292	Crude vegetable materials	12.0	13.4	2.7	16.1	28,550
031	Fresh and preserved fish	7.0	12.6	0.5	13.1	28,334
657	Floor coverings	8.7	14.0	7.0	21.0	16,027
075	Spices	8.9	12.6	0.6	13.2	12,616
656	Articles of textile materials	8.2	11.1	18.6	29.7	10,800
074	Tea and maté	15.9	18.4	0.0	18.4	8,640
071	Coffee	5.4	8.0	0.0	8.0	7,481
011	Fresh or frozen meat	10.5	15.6	6.8	22.4	6,324
611	Leather	4.9	9.4	4.8	14.2	6,161
032	Fish in airtight containers	5.6	12.6	4.7	17.3	4,662
697	Base metal household equipment	12.2	17.6	8.2	25.8	4,602
693	Wire products and fencing grills	9.8	14.2	7.3	21.5	4,380
673	Iron and steel bars	12.0	20.1	5.7	25.8	4,202
851	Footwear	9.2	25.3	8.8	34.1	3,941

Code						
695	Hand tools	6.7	6.7	8.0	14.7	3,524
671	Pig iron	7.9	17.0	2.0	19.0	3,524
422	Other fixed vegetable oils	4.0	10.4	7.3	17.7	3,161
897	Jewelry	3.9	13.7	14.9	28.6	3,113
681	Silver and platinum	0.5	2.1	0.1	2.2	2,850
651	Textile yarn and thread	8.6	26.9	14.8	41.7	2,729
663	Mineral manufactures, n.e.s.*	7.0	8.1	8.6	16.7	2,472
694	Nails, screws, nuts, and bolts	7.3	17.0	5.9	22.9	2,358
654	Lace and embroidery	5.7	9.1	18.4	27.5	2,345
632	Wood manufactures, n.e.s.	8.6	28.4	5.7	34.1	2,313
291	Crude animal materials, n.e.s.	11.0	10.5	2.1	12.6	2,244
512	Organic chemicals	8.3	7.9	11.8	19.7	2,096
276	Other crude materials	12.8	35.7	2.9	38.6	1,909
729	Other electrical machinery	3.2	9.7	7.1	16.8	1,891
612	Leather manufactures	6.2	21.1	5.0	26.1	1,822
831	Travel goods and handbags	10.2	17.1	15.3	32.4	1,649
698	Metal manufactures, n.e.s.	6.8	16.8	8.1	24.9	1,636
284	Nonferrous metal scrap	3.8	37.8	4.6	42.4	1,549
896	Antiques and works of art	1.0	9.3	1.4	10.7	1,382
679	Iron and steel castings	7.8	28.5	8.2	36.7	1,134
283	Ores of nonferrous metals	16.5	52.8	1.1	53.9	1,087
599	Chemical materials, n.e.s.	7.1	17.1	6.8	23.9	1,055
655	Special textile fabrics	9.7	16.1	15.3	31.4	1,046
678	Iron and steel tubes	10.9	15.8	7.2	23.0	1,037
263	Cotton	4.6	17.8	3.1	20.9	1,030
	Median ad valorem rate	7.8	14.2	6.4	20.6	
	Average ad valorem rate	7.4	13.6	7.5	21.1	

*n.e.s. = not elsewhere specified.

Source: Alexander J. Yeats, "A Comparative Analysis of the Incidence of Tariffs and Transportation Costs on India's Exports," Journal of Development Studies 14 (October 1977):100. Reprinted by permission of Frank Cass & Co. Ltd., London.

TABLE 4.3

Comparison of the Ad Valorem Incidence of International Transport and Insurance Charges
for Indonesia's Exports to the United States with Post-Kennedy Round Tariffs

SITC	Description	Average Transport Rate for U.S. Imports	Rate for Indonesian Exports			1974 F.A.S. Value of Exports to the United States ($000)
			Transport Rate	Nominal Tariffs	Total	
331	Crude petroleum	8.0	12.0	4.1	16.1	1,196,814
231	Crude rubber	11.6	10.9	0.6	11.5	213,850
332	Petroleum products	6.8	20.9	2.7	23.6	75,307
071	Coffee	5.4	10.6	0.0	10.6	56,058
422	Other fixed vegetable oils	4.0	5.5	7.3	12.8	33,893
687	Tin	1.5	1.5	5.5	7.0	30,398
075	Spices	8.9	8.4	0.6	9.0	28,939
074	Tea and maté	15.9	18.3	0.0	18.3	12,041
551	Essential oils	2.8	3.8	3.2	7.0	10,785
031	Fresh fish	7.0	10.2	0.5	10.7	8,604
729	Other electrical machinery	3.2	1.5	7.3	8.8	7,291
121	Tobacco, unmanufactured	6.4	36.7	22.7	59.4	1,929
541	Medicinal products	3.3	2.9	4.5	7.4	1,687
632	Wood manufactures, n.e.s.*	8.6	29.7	5.7	35.4	1,590
841	Clothing	8.0	10.4	22.1	32.5	1,120
032	Fish in airtight containers	5.6	12.7	4.7	17.4	747

242	Wood in the rough	7.1	40.1	0.0	40.1	736
243	Wood shaped	7.1	36.0	0.0	36.0	546
421	Fixed vegetable oils	6.2	2.6	7.2	9.8	539
896	Works of art	1.0	6.5	1.2	7.7	314
292	Crude vegetable materials	12.0	38.6	2.7	41.3	311
341	Natural gas	2.7	25.6	0.0	25.6	264
678	Iron and steel pipes	10.9	15.2	7.2	22.4	197
211	Hides and skins	3.9	12.4	0.1	12.5	146
653	Textile fabrics woven	5.8	19.3	19.4	38.7	109
655	Special textile fabrics	9.7	23.1	15.3	38.4	79
053	Preserved fruit	11.5	32.0	12.5	44.5	72
656	Made up textile articles	8.2	32.8	18.6	51.4	69
072	Cocoa	5.4	8.6	1.7	10.3	55
652	Cotton fabrics woven	5.4	34.1	21.1	55.2	55
899	Manufactured articles, n.e.s.	12.0	60.1	12.8	72.9	48
291	Crude animal materials	11.0	19.6	2.1	21.7	47
667	Pearls and precious stones	0.5	1.4	2.5	3.9	34
897	Jewelry	3.9	5.6	14.9	20.5	30
712	Agricultural machinery	11.6	11.0	1.3	12.3	12
892	Printed matter	5.9	46.7	2.3	49.0	11
692	Metal containers	6.2	6.9	6.3	13.2	11
694	Nails, screws, nuts, bolts	7.3	26.0	5.9	31.9	10
099	Food preparations, n.e.s.	15.6	40.0	4.7	44.7	10
631	Plywood and veneers	15.6	20.3	6.0	26.3	9

*n.e.s. = not elsewhere specified.

Source: Alexander J. Yeats, "The Incidence of Transport Costs on Indonesian Exports to the United States," Bulletin of Indonesian Economic Studies 12 (November 1976):66. Reprinted by permission.

on U.S. imports from all countries. The transport charge for Indonesia is higher than average in 35 of the 40 three-digit groups shown. Averaged over all 40 groups, the adverse transport cost differential borne by Indonesian exports is about 12 percentage points, but it reaches up to 20 or 30 points for such important product groups as tobacco, wood, or crude vegetable materials. The adverse differential facing Indonesia's crude petroleum exports is only 4 percentage points, but it is of special significance since it is equivalent to about $50 million in potential foreign exchange earnings.

Indonesia's excess transport costs may be due to its remote location from the U.S. market or to an unfavorable commodity structure of exports, or to other factors that are substantially beyond its control. However, they may also be due to inefficiencies or other potentially correctable factors. Some light may be thrown on this by comparing the incidence of transport costs on Indonesian exports with that on similar products exported by Malaysia. Malaysia lies about the same nautical distance from U.S. ports and exports many of the same types of products as Indonesia. Thus, where similar Indonesian export products have higher transport charges than Malaysian, this may point to inefficiencies and also provide some rough guide to the magnitude of the potential saving in transport costs.

The following procedure was used for such a comparison. First, U.S. import statistics were employed to identify each individual Schedule A product included in the three-digit SITC groups shown in Table 4.3. Next, those items not exported by either Indonesia or Malaysia were deleted from the list and the largest (in terms of Indonesian export values) Schedule A product was selected from each remaining SITC group. Finally, the Malaysian transport rate for each Schedule A product was computed by taking the ratio of the c.i.f. to the f.a.s. value. The sample was made as large as possible, but several of the SITC groups (for example, essential oils, manufactured tobacco, medicinal products) had to be dropped since they were not exported by Malaysia; in other cases the value of shipments of matched Schedule A products was too small for meaningful comparison.

Table 4.4 compares the Indonesian and Malaysian export values and transport rates for the items selected. Since these Schedule A products are narrowly defined, both in terms of product characteristics and by implication in terms of stowage factors, the observed differences in shipping costs may reasonably be attributed to differences in transport facilities and operations (loading or harbor charges, turnaround time, age and efficiency of vessels, competition from nonliners, and so on) or to rate discrimination by shipping conferences.

Overall, Table 4.4 suggests that Indonesian exports bear excess transport costs on shipments to the United States. Of the 22 products shown, 18 have higher ad valorem freight rates for Indonesia. The widest differential is for split bamboo where the transport charge on Indonesian exports is 50 percentage points higher than on Malaysian. Differentials in excess of 10 percentage points appear for hardwood products, pineapples, cloth tableware, and woven cotton. The only instance where the differential is reversed is hardwood logs. Since Indonesia exports about 20 times as much of this product annually as Malaysia, Indonesia's advantage in transport costs in this case may be due to economies of scale in shipping.

In an attempt to summarize the implications of these figures, the Malaysian transport rates were applied to the Indonesian export values. This procedure permits an approximation to the loss in Indonesian foreign exchange due to higher freight factors. Specifically, the value of lost foreign exchange (L) has been estimated using

$$L = \sum_j V_{ij} t_{ij} - \sum_j V_{ij} t_{mj} \qquad\qquad 4.2$$

where t_{ij} and t_{mj} are the Indonesian and Malaysian ad valorem transport rates for product j, while V_{ij} is the Indonesian export value for shipments of product j to the United States. The equation would overstate the foreign exchange loss if exports were carried in Indonesian-owned vessels. Available evidence from sailing schedules, however, indicates that these are little used on the U.S. run.

Application of equation 4.2 to the Indonesian trade data indicates that, had Indonesian exporters been subject to Malaysian ad valorem transport rates for these 22 products, this would have resulted in a reduction in transport costs of \$40 million and foreign exchange savings approaching this figure.*

---

*Using transport cost data compiled from Australian import statistics, Peter Lloyd shows that most of the conclusions concerning transport costs on Indonesia's U.S. exports also hold for this alternative market. First, ad valorem freight costs for exports to Australia averaged over 16 percent, but the average tariff rate was under 1 percent. For similar products shipped, Indonesian transport costs were also generally higher than those from Malaysia, Singapore, or Papua-New Guinea.[9]

TABLE 4.4

Comparison of the Ad Valorem Incidence of Transport Costs on
Similar Products Exported by Indonesia and Malaysia

| Schedule A Number | Description | Value of Exports ($000) | | Transportation Cost Factor | | |
		Indonesia	Malaysia	Indonesia	Malaysia	Difference
3310140	Crude petroleum, 25 degrees API or more	1,113,516.9	15,001.8	12.0	8.9	+3.1
2311050	Rubber natural dry form	201,314.7	164,390.3	10.5	8.5	+2.0
3324020	Fuel oil, under 25 degrees API	30,560.7	4,197.0	16.9	11.4	+5.5.
0711020	Coffee crude	56,056.2	2,017.3	10.5	7.7	+2.8
4222000	Palm oil	24,486.1	64,299.5	5.4	5.3	+0.1
6871020	Tin unwrought	30,339.8	163,691.6	1.5	1.5	—
0751020	Black pepper unground	12,936.2	3,805.8	9.2	8.1	+1.1
0741000	Tea	12,041.3	30.8	18.3	11.2	+7.1
0313070	Shrimps and prawns, shell on	4,506.2	736.2	6.6	8.3	-1.7
7299400	Electrical signaling apparatus	6,830.5	12,229.7	1.4	1.3	+0.2

6328850	Hardwood dowels and pins	1,503.1	11,003.0	29.5	17.3	+12.2
8411191	Other men's cotton apparel	576.5	163.6	5.9	5.3	+0.6
0320243	Shrimp peeled but not breaded	401.4	480.5	16.6	11.1	+5.5
2423050	Hardwood logs except pulpwood	735.6	105.5	40.1	56.9	−16.8
2433155	Rough hardwood lumber	271.3	10,544.9	40.3	34.8	+5.5
8960600	Antiques	168.9	20.7	10.1	8.4	+1.7
2923050	Split bamboo and rattan	129.8	203.5	53.5	4.8	+48.7
3410020	Liquified petroleum gases	264.2	4,958.2	25.6	20.0	+5.6
0538040	Pineapples in airtight containers	71.3	2,365.9	31.7	12.8	+18.9
6569170	Tablecloths and napkins of vegetable fiber	19.9	232.8	20.4	4.6	+15.8
0721000	Cocoa beans	55.3	782.2	8.6	8.6	—
6522597	Bleached or colored woven cotton	53.6	1,714.3	34.7	5.1	+29.6
	Median ad valorem rate			14.3	8.3	+6.0
	Average ad valorem rate*			18.6	11.9	+6.7

*Unweighted average.

Source: Alexander J. Yeats, "The Incidence of Transport Costs on Indonesia's Exports to the United States," Bulletin of Indonesian Economic Studies 12 (November 1976), p. 69. Reprinted by permission.

The transport profiles for India and Indonesia suggest that
shipping costs may pose a far more important barrier to developing
country exports than current MFN tariffs. However, this general
conclusion may be challenged on two points: that ad valorem freight
costs for Asian developing countries such as India or Indonesia are
not typical of those for countries in other regions, and that freight
rates for shipments to the United States (the export market for the
Indian and Indonesian studies) were not representative for shipments
to, say, Europe.

Concerning the first point, an important study by David Brodsky and Gary Sampson has shown that ad valorem transport costs for
Latin American exports to the United States are on the same order
of magnitude as freight costs for the Asian exporters.[10] Table 4.5
summarizes the findings of this investigation and shows the average
ad valorem freight costs facing ten Latin American Free Trade Area
countries (LAFTA) by two-digit SITC groups. The results are notable
both for the magnitude and dispersion of the nominal transport costs.
For example, ad valorem freight rates ranging from 30 to 50 percent
are observed for all LAFTA country shipments of wood, lumber, and
cork products (SITC 24), with freight factors for rubber goods (SITC
62) also being in this range. However, the highest freight factor is
for shipments of Brazilian coal, where transport costs are actually
over 300 percent of the f.a.s. value of the product, while shipments
of furniture (SITC 82) from Chile and Paraguay bear freight factors
in the range of 50 to 70 percent. The results in Table 4.5 show the
conclusion that transport costs pose a more formidable barrier to
exports than tariffs also holds for the LAFTA countries as well as
Asian countries like India and Indonesia.

A second question of importance is whether the same level
of transport costs applies to shipments destined for other developed
country markets. While further research is needed, Carmellah
Moneta has shown that ad valorem freight rates for developing country exports to the Federal Republic of Germany also reach imposing
magnitudes in a number of cases.[11] As an illustration, the aggregate freight factor for Tunisian exports to Germany was found to be
50 percent, while ad valorem transport rates in excess of 30 percent
were recorded for Iraq, Guatemala, Honduras, Spain, Nicaragua,
Venezuela, and Brazil. The Moneta study also concluded that product
value was one of the major determinants of freight rates. This finding, which has been confirmed in subsequent studies, indicates that
the true cost-of-carriage may not generally be reflected in actual

freight rates, and that shipping charges may often discriminate against processed goods.*

Specially Disadvantaged Countries

While the preceding analysis examined the general incidence of ad valorem freight costs on developing country exports, there are a number of developing countries that have special transport problems. Specifically, land-locked countries such as Chad, the Central African Republic, Bolivia, Paraguay, Laos, Bolivia, Afghanistan, and others must ship goods a substantial distance over a neighbor's frontier before reaching a seaport. Given the dimensions of the additional land freight costs involved (which UNCTAD estimates may equal 30 to 60 percent of the f.o.b. export price), it is acknowledged that transportation problems are of major importance for these geographically disadvantaged countries. For example, one consequence is that foreign exchange outlays per unit of exports are generally higher than would be the case if transit through another country were not required.

However, the consequences of a land-locked status may be far more important than this additional loss of foreign exchange. For example, UNCTAD notes that

> the effects of a land-locked situation may be difficult to quantify, if only because societies adapt to their circumstances and those economic activities which are most seriously impeded by the unfavourable transport situation may simply fail to take place and are thus not observable. But current experience as well as history and

---

*An important question centers on whether developing countries gain some bargaining advantage over the conferences as they move from exporters of primary products to semiprocessed and processed goods. Some evidence suggests that such gains may be minimal. For example, studies of the transport cost profiles of Australia and South Africa show that these developed countries, which share the location problems of many developing countries, bear freight rates that on average are two to three times the level of MFN tariffs facing their exports.[12]

TABLE 4.5

The Incidence of Ad Valorem Transport and Insurance Costs on LAFTA Country Exports to the United States
(all figures in percent)

SITC	Product	Argentina	Bolivia	Brazil	Chile	Colombia	Ecuador	Paraguay	Peru	Uruguay	Venezuela
00	Live animals	12	—	—	6	18	12	5	23	8	2
01	Meat and preparations	5	—	4	—	—	—	4	—	—	5
02	Dairy products	12	—	—	—	—	8	—	28	20	6
03	Fish and products	17	—	8	6	7	8	—	28	—	19
04	Cereals and preparations	28	—	28	—	15	45	26	—	—	36
05	Fruits and vegetables	17	8	13	41	44	53	6	14	—	12
06	Sugar and preparations	7	6	6	17	6	5	5	7	8	4
07	Coffee, cocoa, tea, spices	21	6	6	19	4	5	8	5	—	—
08	Animal feeds	15	—	33	90	—	8	21	11	—	9
09	Miscellaneous foods	11	—	40	—	18	—	—	9	—	13
11	Beverages	17	—	119	29	30	—	19	22	—	6
12	Tobacco	10	—	10	—	9	5	6	11	—	5
21	Hides and skins	3	6	7	4	7	6	6	6	—	15
22	Oilseeds	—	—	9	—	15	—	—	—	—	6
23	Crude rubber	—	—	8	—	—	—	—	—	—	—
24	Wood, lumber, and cork	30	31	31	41	46	32	40	47	6	29
26	Textile fibers	6	1	9	40	15	12	—	4	83	3
27	Crude minerals	45	—	18	10	—	—	34	79	—	—
28	Metalliferous ores	4	2	35	20	3	7	—	11	—	40
29	Animal and vegetable material	17	14	14	7	52	27	20	14	18	8
32	Coal and coke	—	—	307	—	—	—	—	—	—	—
33	Petroleum and products	6	7	10	2	7	6	—	9	—	6
34	Gas	—	—	—	—	—	—	—	—	—	14
41	Animal oils and fats	—	—	4	—	—	—	7	—	—	—
42	Vegetable oils and fats	9	—	5	—	—	—	—	—	—	—

Code	Commodity	1	2	3	4	5	6	7	8	9	10
43	Fatty acids	14	—	5	3	7	—	—	—	—	—
51	Chemical elements	11	—	4	1	4	12	—	3	19	9
53	Dyeing materials	21	—	14	—	—	—	22	32	—	14
54	Medicinal products	7	—	6	4	4	—	—	1	5	17
55	Toilet preparations	4	—	4	5	8	—	4	2	4	11
56	Manufactured fertilizer	11	—	17	6	18	—	—	—	—	—
57	Explosives	6	—	15	—	—	—	—	58	—	35
58	Plastic materials	23	—	12	9	9	—	—	—	—	12
59	Chemicals, n.e.s. *	7	—	6	—	6	—	—	—	9	—
61	Leather goods	5	6	5	10	5	—	7	3	7	4
62	Rubber goods	8	42	43	—	5	—	—	27	—	33
63	Wood and cork	17	30	24	23	20	21	4	50	7	24
64	Paper	32	—	29	22	14	5	5	17	—	13
65	Textile yarn	6	12	7	5	5	—	26	4	4	4
66	Mineral manufactures	17	9	7	21	6	14	2	18	20	8
67	Iron and steel	11	—	10	—	12	—	—	—	—	11
68	Nonferrous metals	32	1	11	2	1	—	—	3	—	9
69	Metal manufacutres, n.e.s.	9	6	11	8	11	28	22	7	30	17
71	Nonelectrical machinery	9	—	6	6	10	7	—	35	8	17
72	Electrical machinery	9	—	7	5	16	7	—	—	—	10
73	Transport equipment	13	—	24	3	14	—	—	19	—	19
81	Plumbing fixtures	24	—	28	—	12	—	—	—	—	—
82	Furniture	16	16	16	52	16	33	70	20	—	26
83	Travel goods	7	16	9	9	6	7	14	7	7	6
84	Clothing and accessories	5	9	10	22	5	8	20	7	4	5
85	Footwear	12	8	10	12	6	34	18	30	10	4
86	Scientific instruments	8	3	6	9	5	8	11	5	—	6
89	Miscellaneous manufactures	30	9	12	1	9	7	8	3	1	3

*n.e.s. = not elsewhere specified.

Source: David Brodsky and Gary Sampson, "International Transport and Latin American Exports to the United States," International Journal of Transport Economics 7 (December 1979):283. Reprinted by permission.

common sense point to a lack of seashores as a substantial handicap in economic and social development. Overall growth, whether through import substitution, export expansion, or the utilization of foreign capital resources, gives rise to demands for international transport services. The greater difficulty and costs of such services for land-locked countries thus constitutes an extra hurdle to their development.[13]

The required usage of another country's transportation facilities may compound these disadvantaged nations' trade problems in other ways. For example, the land-locked countries often find themselves almost totally dependent on another country's transport policy, transport enterprises, and transport facilities. This raises the possibility of monopolistic exploitation, irrespective of whether practiced deliberately in the pricing of transport facilities or in the limitation of access to transport routes. Furthermore, dependence on the transit country's transport facilities also entails a lack of control over the development of the infrastructure, transport management, and policy, which normally is shaped by the transit country in response to its own economic and social interests.

While it is acknowledged that the problems of individual land-locked countries have distinctly different features, UNCTAD has proposed guidelines to alleviate these transport difficulties. Essentially, these guidelines cover three major problem areas: the improvement of transiting procedures and regulations by joint action, joint ventures in transport projects, and rules concerning pricing of transport services.

Concerning the first point, UNCTAD suggests that specific attention be directed to methods for investigating and evaluating procedural impediments along the main routes of transit serving land-locked countries. The objective is to identify unnecessary transit procedures that impede the trade of the land-locked country. Furthermore, the analysis of transit procedures should extend to both the rules being applied and the methods of application. In particular, special note was made of the necessity of improving customs procedures and trade facilitation methods as they influence land-locked countries.

With regard to joint ventures, several specific proposals were stressed. Here the development of economic policy guidelines, including, if possible, model codes for joint ventures in the field of transport, are given special importance. In particular, these guidelines were intended to cover methods for identifying and analyzing projects; methods for sharing costs and benefits that take account of changing circumstances, including changes in the size and incidence of costs and benefits; special provisions for the sharing of costs and benefits in continuing and periodic activities (such as carrier operations, management, or maintenance of facilities and equipment); and the provision of a guide to national and feasible systems of economic accounting for transport activities of different types.

Finally, it was felt that the pricing of transport services required by land-locked developing countries should be another area subject to international policy guidelines. Here it was noted that developing land-locked and transit countries together are generally affected by transport prices set outside their control. These externally determined prices and freight tariffs may contain irrationalities that harm the developing countries without helping the international transport interests (see Chapter 3). Guidelines are required for the international community concerning the pricing of transport services and other detriments to the trade of these specially disadvantaged countries.

THE INTERACTION OF TARIFFS AND TRANSPORT COSTS

Aside from the question of levels, transport costs have an important indirect effect on developing country exports, in general, and on land-locked countries, in particular. For example, when establishing the value of imports for tariff assessment, two alternative procedures have been employed in determining the base to which nominal tariffs are applied. The European countries and Japan employ a c.i.f. valuation base under which tariffs are applied to the selling price in the exporting country, plus all transportation and insurance charges involved in bringing the goods to the port of entry in the importing market. In contrast, the United States, Canada, and Australia use an f.o.b. procedure for establishing the valuation base. Under this system, nominal tariffs are applied to the f.o.b. price of exports exclusive of the cost of transport and insurance to the port of entry in the importing country.

Several previous studies have examined the possible effects of these alternative valuation procedures within the context of theoretical models of international trade flows.[14] These investigations have correctly noted that a c.i.f. valuation base places a disproportionate burden on countries that experience relatively higher freight costs. If transport costs are related to distance, nations that are not favorably located in relation to their major export markets bear disproportionate tariff costs relative to their competitors. In contrast, the f.o.b. valuation procedure does not penalize potential exporters for locational disadvantages, but applies a nominal tariff rate directly to the export price in each individual country.

Geographic considerations, as well as technological factors in shipping, place many developing countries at a competitive disadvantage in relation to industrial nations that are normally better located in relation to their export markets. As such, the c.i.f. valuation procedure places a disproportionate tariff burden on some developing countries that must already overcome higher transportation costs. However, a lack of comprehensive empirical data on shipping costs borne by developed and developing countries has prevented any quantitative assessment of the regressive impact of a c.i.f. valuation base.

Economic Consequences of the Valuation Base

The preceding points concerning the effects of alternative tariff valuation procedures can be illustrated through recourse to an algebraic example. In a situation where an f.o.b. tariff (t) is applied to imports, the duty paid (d_f) by an exporting country is equal to

$$d_f = p_b t \qquad\qquad 4.3$$

where p_b is the f.o.b. price of the good. Under a c.i.f. system, the tariff rate is applied to the f.o.b. price plus all transport and insurance costs incurred in bringing the good to the importing country. If the importer were to shift from an f.o.b. to a c.i.f. valuation base, the percentage point increase in import duties could be approximated from

$$\frac{\Delta d}{p_b} = \frac{p_b t + ftp_b - p_b t}{p_b} = ft \qquad\qquad 4.4$$

where f represents ad valorem transport and insurance costs.

In addition to this increase in the level of import duties, there would be varying effects on different exporters. For reasons relating to such factors as distance, quality of transport services available, or volume of goods shipped, freight costs for similar products will differ from country to country. Shifting from an f.o.b. to a c.i.f. valuation base would have a detrimental impact on the export performance of high transport cost countries since the increase in their tariffs would be greater than that for other nations.

Consider the case where a manufactured good is exported by a developing to a developed country. In the normal case where the developing country is a residual supplier in international markets, its f.o.b. export price is determined by the domestic price in the industrial market (P) less transportation charges per unit (R) and tariffs. With an f.o.b. tariff valuation this price (p_{bb}) equals

$$p_{bb} = P - R - p_{bb}t \qquad\qquad 4.5$$

or

$$p_{bb} = P/(1 + f + t) \qquad\qquad 4.6$$

However, under a c.i.f. valuation system the developing country export price (p_{bc}) is derived from a different equality:

$$p_{bc} = P - R - (p_{bc} + R)t \qquad\qquad 4.7$$

which indicates

$$p_{bc} = P/(1 + f + t + ft) \qquad\qquad 4.8$$

The percentage price change in developing country exports accompanying a shift from an f.o.b. to a c.i.f. base could therefore be approximated from

$$\frac{p_{bc} - p_{bb}}{p_{bb}} = \frac{(1 + f + t)}{(1 + f + t + ft)} - 1 \qquad\qquad 4.9$$

Since the U.S. import statistics now permit separate estimation of transport and insurance costs (see Chapter 2), these data were used to approximate the increases in import duties and price effects of a shift from an f.o.b. to a c.i.f. tariff base. In these simulations an attempt was made to estimate the effects on developing countries in six geographic regions: the Near East, Central Asia, South Asia, South America, East Africa, and North Africa. Ad valorem freight rates for exports from Israel, India, the Philippines, and Brazil were employed as proxies for the first four regions, while Kenya or Ethiopia was used for East Africa, and Tunisia or Egypt for North Africa. However, the limited range of exports from African countries necessitated substitutions in some cases.

Table 4.6 shows ad valorem freight costs for a random sample of 35 four-digit SITC manufactured products exported to the United States. These items were drawn from a list of labor-intensive manufactures whose production characteristics were judged to make them

TABLE 4.6

Analysis of the Incidence of Transportation Costs on Products of Export Interest to Developing Countries

SITC	Description	Africa		Near East	Asia		South America	Industrial Countries
		East	North		Central	South		
0053	Canned fruits and vegetables	14.8	18.0	23.9	19.9	20.1	16.1	14.8
0055	Dehydrated fruits	29.2	14.6	17.3	23.0	16.5	21.9	17.2
0062	Confectionary	40.6	n.a.	16.7	15.7	18.2	18.9	11.9
1221	Cigars*	n.a.	18.7	30.4	77.4	9.7	9.6	12.2
2433	Hardwood flooring	n.a.	31.9	n.a.	16.4	42.0	33.3	10.8
6310	Veneers and plywood	n.a.	45.8	22.2	36.3	32.5	27.9	6.5
6320	Prefabricated wood structures	26.9	37.5	8.1	28.4	23.5	17.4	10.3
6421	Nontextile bags and boxes	n.a.	n.a.	n.a.	16.5	114.9	28.9	15.9
6532	Broad woven wool mills	19.5	39.2	12.5	13.8	6.4	7.3	5.0
6535	Broad woven fabrics	n.a.	6.0	9.1	15.2	24.8	5.5	7.1
6540	Narrow fabric mills	n.a.	8.1	8.3	9.1	27.6	12.1	7.2
6550	Lace goods	9.8	27.3	19.1	18.0	10.8	5.1	6.2
6556	Cordage	9.8	29.4	n.a.	33.2	11.1	5.1	5.4
6561	Textile bags	21.0	n.a.	n.a.	16.5	69.8	3.6	12.8
6569	Tire cord	30.4	15.6	7.2	16.4	18.6	7.8	11.4

Code	Product						
6930	Fabricated wire products	n.a.	n.a.	7.0	14.2	9.7	15.0	5.7
6981	Hardware, n.e.s.	n.a.	13.1	5.8	12.1	11.1	10.6	7.7
7196	Other machinery	n.a.	n.a.	2.7	25.7	10.9	9.5	5.7
7232	Porcelain electrical supplies	n.a.	n.a.	n.a.	38.9	11.6	6.2	10.9
7250	Electric housewares	13.0	n.a.	19.3	13.6	10.2	26.3	7.1
8124	Lighting fixtures	7.9	37.0	5.7	24.0	29.3	52.7	8.3
8210	Wood furniture	13.1	15.6	12.6	40.5	51.9	15.5	16.2
8310	Luggage	23.4	10.6	9.0	17.1	18.8	8.6	9.1
8411	Men's suits and coats	28.5	16.0	9.7	15.0	8.4	9.9	7.3
8413	Leather gloves	n.a.	n.a.	n.a.	33.2	10.6	7.0	4.9
8414	Robes and dressing gowns	30.8	17.6	8.7	15.9	13.1	12.2	4.2
8510	Rubber footwear	n.a.	n.a.	23.3	13.0	17.0	12.2	7.2
8612	Ophthalmic goods	n.a.	n.a.	6.6	25.6	8.8	9.8	3.2
8617	Medical instruments	n.a.	n.a.	9.6	23.3	9.2	7.0	4.3
8930	Miscellaneous plastic products	28.2	6.7	10.0	17.0	14.8	10.3	9.9
8940	Games and toys	11.7	7.9	17.7	21.3	13.8	14.2	7.6
8972	Costume jewelry	55.7	11.8	9.2	16.7	19.7	8.2	6.2
8992	Brooms and brushes	72.3	38.3	12.4	38.4	27.3	23.9	6.9
8994	Umbrellas	24.2	n.a.	n.a.	24.4	9.7	16.5	7.4
8999	Other manufactures	31.6	n.a.	8.8	14.5	24.2	18.7	8.8
	Average ad valorem rate	25.8	21.2	12.6	22.9	22.2	14.7	8.7

n.a. = not available.

Ad valorem transport rates for shipments of central Asian cigarettes have been used as a proxy for this product.

Source: Alexander J. Yeats, "Tariff Valuation, Transport Costs and the Establishment of Trade Preferences Among Developing Countries," World Development 8 (February 1980):133. Reprinted by permission.

especially suitable for developing countries.[15] Average transport
costs for two industrial countries, the United Kingdom and Germany,
are also shown in an attempt to determine if developing countries
face systematic adverse freight rate differentials.

By region, the average freight rates for shipments of these
manufactured goods ranges from a high of 25.8 percent for East
African exports down to 12.6 percent for the Near East. However,
there is considerable variation from these figures on a product-by-
product basis. South Asian exports of nontextile bags and boxes
(SITC 6421) have an ad valorem freight rate of 115 percent, while
brooms and brushes from East Africa and Central Asian cigars have
freight factors of over 70 percent. The fact that more than one-third
of the products have freight factors of over 20 percent also accents
the potential importance of shipping costs as a trade barrier for
these manufactured goods.

Comparison of developing country ad valorem freight rates
with those for the industrial countries (Germany and United Kingdom)
indicates that developing countries systematically pay higher nominal
shipping costs. Overall, the average industrial country freight factor (8.7 percent) is one-third that for East African exports, and about
60 percent lower than that borne by shipments from Central and South
Asia. Product-by-product comparisons show that developed country
freight factors equal to or lower than corresponding developing
country rates for almost 90 percent of the items, with differentials
of 10 percentage points or more occurring for products such as plywood and veneers, prefabricated wood structures, or robes and gowns.
These findings imply that developing countries may not be advised to
move into production of many high unskilled labor input items unless
such sizable adverse transportation cost differentials can be overcome.*

---

*Several factors could account for the systematic adverse
differentials. If developing countries export inferior quality and
lower price items, shipping costs will constitute a higher percentage
of product price. The fact that many developing countries are less
favorably located than industrial competitors may be a factor to the
extent that freight costs are influenced by distance. A recent study
also notes that transport innovations may have made industrial countries more efficient in shipping and widened the freight cost differential between industrial countries and developing countries. Since

Table 4.7 examines the potential influence of transportation costs on the export position of developing countries if the United States were to shift from an f.o.b. to a c.i.f. tariff base. Shown here are post-Kennedy Round f.o.b. tariffs for these manufactured goods and a simulation (via equation 4.4) of the increase in import duties that would occur if the United States were to apply tariffs inclusive of transportation and insurance charges. Estimates are also given for the price reductions (equation 4.9) required for developing country products to remain competitive with those of U.S. producers. To assist in evaluating the overall implications of a shift to a c.i.f. system, estimates of the average tariff and price changes have been computed for the six developing country regions.

Overall, a c.i.f. valuation base would have the greatest impact on East African exports, where tariffs would rise by about 4 percentage points—an increase of 26 percent. Average increases in import duties of over 20 percent would also be experienced by Central and South Asian countries, as well as North Africa. The implications of these figures can be assessed by noting that the Kennedy Round negotiations produced tariff cuts that averaged 36 percent. Should the United States abandon current practices and include transport charges in the tariff base, as is done in the European countries and Japan, this would offset approximately 60 percent of the average Kennedy Round reduction. In contrast, increases borne by industrial countries would be far less (about 60 percent lower) than those for the developing countries due to their generally

---

competitive pressures in developed countries are stronger, I. Little, T. Scitovsky, and M. Scott suggest that

> containers and other forms of innovation in transport will be introduced there first and will not spread to developing countries' trade for a long time. These innovations might be accompanied by a fundamental change in the whole system of rate fixing, since it would seem rational to base the charge on the container rather than on its contents. The result might be a big reduction in freight on exports of manufactures between developed countries, putting exports from developing countries at a severe disadvantage where the freight element is important.[16]

TABLE 4.7

Analysis of the Tariff Increase and Price Effects of a Shift in the U.S. Valuation Base
from a Free-on-Board to a Cost-Insurance-Freight Procedure

| | | Increase in Import Duties (points) | | | | | | Price Effects on Exports (percent) | | | | | |
| | | Africa | | Near | Asia | | South | Africa | | Near | Asia | | South |
SITC	FOB Tariff	East	North	East	Central	South	America	East	North	East	Central	South	America
0053	12.4	1.8	2.2	3.0	2.5	2.5	2.0	-1.4	-1.7	-2.1	-1.8	-1.9	-1.5
0055	10.2	3.0	1.5	1.8	2.4	1.7	2.2	-2.1	-1.2	-1.4	-1.7	-1.3	-1.7
0062	12.4	5.0	n.a.	2.1	2.0	2.3	2.3	-3.2	n.a.	-1.6	-1.5	-1.7	-1.8
1221	31.4	n.a.	5.9	9.6	24.3	3.1	3.0	n.a.	-3.8	-5.6	-10.4	-2.1	-2.1
2433	7.9	n.a.	2.5	n.a.	1.3	3.3	2.6	n.a.	-1.8	n.a.	-1.0	-2.2	-1.8
6310	9.8	n.a.	4.5	2.2	3.6	3.2	2.7	n.a.	-2.8	-1.6	-2.4	-2.2	-2.0
6320	7.7	2.1	2.9	0.6	2.2	1.8	1.3	-1.5	-2.0	-0.5	-1.6	-1.4	-1.1
6421	13.1	n.a.	n.a.	n.a.	2.2	15.1	3.8	n.a.	n.a.	n.a.	-1.6	-6.2	-2.6
6532	20.0	3.9	7.8	2.5	2.8	1.3	1.5	-2.7	-4.7	-1.9	-2.0	-1.0	-1.1
6535	16.0	n.a.	1.0	1.5	2.4	4.0	0.9	n.a.	-0.8	-1.2	-1.8	-2.7	-0.7
6540	12.8	n.a.	1.0	1.1	1.2	3.5	1.6	n.a.	-0.9	-0.9	-1.0	-2.5	-1.2
6550	19.1	1.9	5.2	3.7	3.4	2.1	1.0	-1.4	-3.4	-2.6	-2.5	-1.6	-0.8
6556	13.3	1.3	3.9	n.a.	4.4	1.5	0.7	-1.1	-2.7	n.a.	-2.9	-1.2	-0.6
6561	16.4	3.4	n.a.	n.a.	2.7	11.5	0.6	-2.5	n.a.	n.a.	-2.0	-5.8	-0.5
6569	20.3	6.2	3.2	1.5	3.3	3.8	1.6	-3.9	-2.3	-1.1	-2.4	-2.7	-1.2

Code												
6930	7.4	n.a.	n.a.	0.5	1.0	0.7	1.1	n.a.	n.a.	-0.5	-0.9	-0.6	-0.9
6981	13.8	n.a.	1.8	0.8	1.7	1.5	1.5	n.a.	-1.4	-0.7	-1.3	-1.2	-1.2
7196	8.4	n.a.	n.a.	0.2	2.2	0.9	0.8	n.a.	n.a.	-0.2	-1.6	-0.8	-0.7
7232	9.6	n.a.	n.a.	n.a.	3.7	1.1	0.6	n.a.	n.a.	n.a.	-2.5	-0.9	-0.5
7250	8.3	1.1	n.a.	1.6	1.1	0.9	2.2	-0.9	n.a.	-1.2	-0.9	-0.7	-1.6
8124	13.6	1.1	5.0	0.8	3.3	4.0	7.2	-0.9	-3.2	-0.7	-2.3	-2.7	-4.1
8210	9.1	1.2	1.4	1.2	3.7	4.7	1.4	-1.0	-1.1	-0.9	-2.4	-2.9	-1.1
8310	12.8	3.0	1.4	1.2	2.2	2.4	1.1	-2.2	-1.1	-0.9	-1.7	-1.8	-0.9
8411	18.0	5.1	2.9	1.8	2.7	1.5	1.8	-3.4	-2.1	-1.4	-2.0	-2.1	-1.4
8413	23.4	n.a.	n.a.	n.a.	7.8	2.5	1.6	n.a.	n.a.	n.a.	-4.7	-1.8	-1.2
8414	18.0	5.5	3.2	1.6	2.9	2.4	2.2	-3.6	-2.3	-1.2	-2.1	-1.8	-1.7
8510	14.9	n.a.	n.a.	3.5	1.9	2.5	1.8	n.a.	n.a.	-2.5	-1.5	-1.9	-1.4
8612	16.0	n.a.	n.a.	1.1	4.1	1.4	1.6	n.a.	n.a.	-0.9	-2.8	-1.1	-1.2
8617	11.0	n.a.	n.a.	1.1	2.6	1.0	0.8	n.a.	n.a.	-0.9	-1.9	-0.8	-0.7
8930	9.4	2.7	0.6	0.9	1.6	1.4	1.0	-1.9	-0.5	-0.8	-1.3	-1.1	-0.8
8940	11.6	1.4	0.9	2.1	2.5	1.6	1.7	-1.1	-0.8	-1.6	-1.8	-1.3	-1.3
8972	14.1	7.9	1.7	1.3	2.4	2.6	1.2	-4.4	-1.3	-1.0	-1.8	-2.0	-0.9
8992	22.5	16.3	8.6	2.8	8.6	6.1	5.4	-7.7	-5.0	-2.0	-5.1	-3.9	-3.5
8994	16.9	4.1	n.a.	n.a.	4.1	1.6	2.8	-2.8	n.a.	n.a.	-2.8	-1.3	-2.1
8999	11.8	3.7	n.a.	1.0	1.7	2.9	2.2	-2.5	n.a.	-0.9	-1.3	-2.1	-1.7
Average percent change	25.8	21.2	12.6	22.9	22.2	14.7		-2.5	-2.1	-1.4	-2.3	-2.0	-1.4
Average change (points)	3.9	3.1	1.9	3.5	3.0	1.9							

Source: Andrzej Olechowski and Alexander Yeats, "Hidden Preferences for Developing Countries: A Note on the U.S. Import Valuation Procedure," Quarterly Review of Economics and Business 19 (Autumn 1979):93. Reprinted by permission.

lower freight costs. In other words, an f.o.b. valuation system off-
sets the competitive disadvantage many developing countries would
experience under a c.i.f. tariff base.*

Analysis of the tariff and price effects on a product-by-product
basis also illustrates the adverse competitive impact of a c.i.f. tariff valuation procedure for many developing country manufactured
goods. For example, inclusion of transport and insurance costs in
the valuation base would increase duties on Central Asian cigars by
24 percentage points (almost 80 percent) and lower exporters' prices
by 10 percent. Tariffs on textile and nontextile bags (SITC 6421 and
6561) from South Asian countries would rise by more than 10 percentage points, while duties on East African brooms and brushes
(SITC 8992) would increase by 16 points. These and other tariff
price changes indicate that many developing country manufactured
products now imported by the United States would be placed at a
serious competitive disadvantage if a c.i.f. valuation practice were
used for imports.†

---

*UNCTAD has made several studies of ways to offset the geo-
graphic handicap facing land-locked developing countries. The results of the simulations shown in Table 4.7 have special implications
for these countries. Since the U.S. import statistics show that land-
locked developing countries normally pay considerably higher freight
costs than other developing countries, use of a c.i.f. tariff base by
European countries and Japan constrains the growth of these countries' exports.

†If a c.i.f. valuation base results in a systematic bias against
developing countries, one would expect the European Economic Community (EEC) to import a lower percentage of total manufactured
goods from developing countries than the United States. Analysis of
actual trade data supports this contention. In 1970 the United States
imported 10 percent of total manufactures from developing countries,
while this figure had climbed to 16 percent by 1976. In contrast, the
EEC imported only 4 percent of total manufactures from developing
countries in 1970 and 5 percent in 1976. However, there are other
elements in the EEC tariff structure that provide a bias against developing country exports. Since a protocol grants duty-free entry
between the EEC and the European Free Trade Association (EFTA)
for many manufactured products, the EEC's common external tariff
for nonpreferential imports now applies only to developing countries,
the United States, Japan, and several other industrial nations.

Policy Conclusions

Several important policy conclusions emerge from these findings. First, by adopting the principle of the Generalized System of Preferences (GSP), developed nations and socialist countries of Europe accepted the proposition that developing countries should receive preferential access to their markets. However, Tables 4.6 and 4.7 show that a c.i.f. tariff valuation system discriminates against developing countries due to the higher transport charges paid by these countries.[17] Furthermore, it was noted that freight costs for the least developed land-locked countries were above average for the developing country group, so the c.i.f. valuation system has a doubly repressive effect on these countries' exports. As such, equity considerations as well as desire to stimulate exports and industrialization of developing countries argue in favor of replacement of c.i.f. valuation procedures with an f.o.b. tariff base.[18]

Aside from the interaction between transport costs and tariffs, the magnitudes of the freight factors revealed in Table 4.6 also have important implications for comparative advantage and development policy. The products chosen for this analysis had previously been identified as having _production_ characteristics that made them especially suitable for developing countries. Yet the fact that many of these items have freight factors that range from 20 to 50 percent or more may negate the advantages developing countries have in the export of these goods. As such, a key question concerns the extent to which appropriate policy measures can offset the negative effects of transport costs. Chapter 6 in this book is addressed to this key consideration.

APPENDIX

On the Use of F.O.B.-C.I.F. Export-Import Statistics for Approximating International Transportation Costs

On various occasions in the past, economists have had cause to compare reported export data, normally valued at f.o.b. prices, with matched c.i.f. import statistics of the trading partner. In many cases the purpose of these comparisons was to obtain a gauge of the relative importance of transport and insurance costs as barriers to international trade. While it has been acknowledged that a number of important data problems may cause serious distortions in the underlying statistics, some researchers have presumed that these were not sufficient to distort the basic influence of freight costs as an explanatory factor for differences in exporter (f.o.b.)-importer (c.i.f.) statistics.[19] The issue is of considerable importance since, if the matched trade data do provide a useful gauge of the incidence of international transport costs, such statistics could be a rich source of information on international transport barriers to trade.

Since the United States now separately tabulates the transport and insurance component of its imports, at very low levels of product detail, these data can be used to decompose bilateral trade statistics into a transport-insurance factor and a residual element (which largely reflects variations in the quality of the data). Specifically, the total observed variation (V_t) between the U.S. c.i.f. import (C_i) and partner country f.o.b. export statistics (F_e) can now be decomposed into a transport factor and residual element

$$V_t = (C_i - F_u)/C_i + (F_u - F_e)/C_i \qquad\qquad 4A.1$$

where F_u is the U.S. f.o.b. valuation of imports, and F_e is the exporter's reported value. The residual element (right-hand term) in the above can be used as a measure of accuracy of the trade data.

Using the procedure indicated by equation 4A.1, Table 4A.1 presents results when total exports of 55 developing countries were matched with corresponding U.S. import statistics. Shown here are each country's reported (f.o.b.) exports, along with the U.S. joint f.o.b. and c.i.f. import values. The three right-hand columns show, in reverse order, the total difference (in percentage points) between U.S. c.i.f. values and partner country f.o.b. exports, the freight factor for each exporting country, and the unexplained difference between partner country and U.S. f.o.b. values. Similar results for 29 developed market economy and socialist countries are shown in Table 4A.2.

On an overall basis, the total variation in the developing country trade data ranges from Kuwait's overstating exports by approximately 250 percent to Egypt's and Sierra Leone's under-reported shipments by about 85 percent.[*] In the case of Kuwait,

---

[*] The Egyptian-U.S. differential is due primarily to the USSR cotton purchase agreement with Egypt. Cotton may be loaded in Soviet vessels in Alexandria and sold (frequently at higher prices

the discrepancy is almost entirely due to problems in valuing petroleum, and the fact that petroleum exports originally destined for the United States were diverted en route. Similar difficulties with petroleum shipments were the primary reason why Bahrain over-reported U.S. exports by about 80 percent.

A fact emerging from Table 4A.1 is that some seemingly high c.i.f.-f.o.b. ratios are largely explained by high transportation and insurance costs. For example, the observed differential for Surinam (21.9 percent) is almost entirely due to freight charges, which account for 21.4 percent of the total c.i.f. value of exports. The reason for such a high freight factor is Surinam's export concentration in a number of bulky low-value items such as scrap metal ores (over 70 percent of total exports) and some basic manufactures. Divergences of 10 percent or more between the reported c.i.f. and f.o.b. values for Taiwan, Chile, Iran, Liberia, and Guatemala can also be explained by the existence of nominal transport costs that range between 10 and 17 percent of the c.i.f. export value. However, even when the existence of transport and insurance charges are accounted for, 20 of these 55 countries have a residual variation of more than 20 percent in their trade statistics.

Table 4A.2 shows similar data for the developed and socialist countries. Only three of the 29 countries—South Africa, Austria, and Romania—have an unexplained residual that averages over 20 percent of c.i.f. exports, while the trade data for almost 40 percent of the developing countries shown in Table 4A.1 exceeded this figure. Another fact emerging from Table 4A.2 is that the developed countries have a lower overall freight factor (6.7 percent of c.i.f. exports or 7.2 percent of the f.o.b. value) than the developing nations.

A question of key importance for transport economists is whether normal export-import ratios provide useful approximations to the ad valorem incidence of shipping costs. As noted, several previous studies have assumed that the f.o.b.-c.i.f. ratios do reflect transport and insurance charges, even though there have been no direct tests of this association.

---

than paid to the Egyptians) in other markets. After loading, the Egyptians may not be aware of the final destination for their produce. Illicit trade in diamonds is a major factor in Sierra Leone's understatement of exports.

TABLE 4A.1

Analysis of the Relation between U.S. 1974 Import Values and Developing Country Trading Partners' Reported F.O.B. Exports

Exporting Country	Exporter's F.O.B. Value ($000,000)	U.S. Import Value ($000,000)		Decomposition of C.I.F.–F.O.B. Differences (percentage points)		
		Free Alongside Ship	Cost-Insurance-Freight	Unexplained Variation	Transport Costs	Total Variation
Kuwait	55.3	13.4	15.4	-272.1	13.0	-259.1
Tunisia	47.4	21.5	23.8	-110.1	9.7	-100.4
Bahrain	129.3	60.7	70.4	-97.4	13.8	-83.7
Singapore	862.6	550.4	584.2	-53.4	5.8	-47.7
Bahamas	1,303.5	957.0	1,003.0	-34.5	4.6	-30.0
Jamaica	339.2	234.1	267.8	-39.2	12.6	-26.7
Israel	305.6	281.3	295.9	-8.2	4.9	-3.3
Trinidad	1,371.0	1,271.8	1,346.3	-7.4	5.5	-1.8
Philippines	1,133.1	1,083.9	1,192.7	-4.1	9.1	5.0
Netherlands Antilles	2,018.6	2,009.3	2,133.0	-0.4	5.8	5.4
Korea	1,492.2	1,444.8	1,583.7	-3.0	8.8	5.8
Colombia	517.4	511.0	549.4	-1.2	7.0	5.8
Brazil	1,737.0	1,699.9	1,853.2	-2.0	8.3	6.3
Algeria	1,091.1	1,090.5	1,169.6	-0.1	6.8	6.7
Thailand	195.8	184.2	210.2	-5.5	12.4	6.9
Venezuela	4,680.0	4,671.1	5,037.3	-0.2	7.3	7.1

Angola	372.6	378.1	409.8	1.3	7.7	9.1
China–Taiwan	2,052.9	2,097.7	2,306.9	1.9	9.1	11.0
Hong Kong	1,573.5	1,640.0	1,778.5	3.7	7.8	11.5
Dominican Republic	442.5	473.3	502.5	6.1	5.8	11.9
Chile	286.1	310.3	325.1	7.4	4.6	12.0
Iran	2,133.0	2,132.2	2,459.8	-0.0	13.3	13.3
Saudi Arabia	1,671.0	1,671.2	1,926.5	0.0	13.3	13.3
Panama	103.5	106.2	119.7	2.3	11.3	13.5
Honduras	149.3	149.2	176.6	-0.1	15.5	15.5
Indonesia	1,580.3	1,688.1	1,887.8	5.7	10.6	16.3
Peru	543.5	608.7	650.4	10.0	6.4	16.4
Ivory Coast	85.6	95.3	102.7	9.4	7.2	16.7
Guatemala	188.3	210.4	229.7	9.6	8.4	18.0
Liberia	94.8	96.4	115.7	1.4	16.7	18.1
Sri Lanka	39.0	40.8	48.0	3.7	15.0	18.8
Ecuador	430.5	473.0	527.3	8.1	10.3	18.4
Morocco	18.1	19.3	22.4	5.4	13.8	19.2
India	508.3	559.5	635.2	8.1	11.9	20.0
Argentina	334.2	385.8	418.5	12.3	7.8	20.1
Malagasy Republic	50.3	60.0	64.3	15.1	6.7	21.8
Surinam	73.9	74.4	94.6	0.5	21.4	21.9
Pakistan	51.8	60.7	67.7	13.1	10.3	23.5
Guyana	68.1	83.2	93.5	16.1	11.0	27.2
Costa Rica	142.1	168.5	195.5	13.5	13.8	27.3
Malaysia	595.4	769.7	820.6	21.2	6.2	27.4
El Salvador	121.1	160.6	168.8	23.4	4.9	28.3
Nigeria	2,522.5	3,286.2	3,541.1	21.6	7.2	28.8

(continued)

TABLE 4A.1 (continued)

Exporting Country	Exporter's F.O.B. Value ($000,000)	U.S. Import Value ($000,000)		Decomposition of C.I.F.–F.O.B. Differences (percentage points)		
		Free Alongside Ship	Cost-Insurance-Freight	Unexplained Variation	Transport Costs	Total Variation
Mauritius	24.6	31.8	34.9	20.6	8.9	29.5
Nicaragua	73.7	97.4	108.4	21.9	10.1	32.0
Cameroon	19.1	26.5	28.1	26.3	5.7	32.0
Barbados	22.0	31.8	33.9	28.9	6.2	35.1
Bangladesh	52.4	68.0	81.2	19.2	16.3	35.5
Mozambique	31.7	44.9	50.0	26.4	10.2	36.6
Ghana	85.3	125.5	136.8	29.4	8.3	37.6
Kenya	22.2	39.5	44.1	39.2	10.4	49.7
Mexico	1,667.5	3,390.4	3,446.4	50.0	1.6	51.6
Haiti	48.2	111.2	118.0	53.4	5.8	59.2
Egypt	11.6	69.7	82.9	70.1	15.9	86.0
Sierra Leone	8.2	65.0	65.6	86.6	0.9	87.5
Total	35,578.1	37,985.4	41,255.4	5.8	7.9	13.7

Source: Alexander J. Yeats, "On the Accuracy of Partner Country Trade Statistics," Oxford Bulletin of Economics and Statistics 40 (November 1978):342. Reprinted by permission.

TABLE 4A.2

Analysis of the Relation between U.S. 1974 Import Values and Developed Country Trading Partners Reported F.O.B. Exports

Exporting Country	Exporter's F.O.B. Value ($000,000)	U.S. Import Value ($000,000)		Decomposition of C.I.F.-F.O.B. Differences (percentage points)		
		Free Alongside Ship	Cost-Insurance-Freight	Unexplained Variation	Transport Costs	Total Variation
Yugoslavia	315.7	266.9	286.6	-17.0	6.9	-10.2
Norway	333.2	306.4	327.7	-8.2	6.5	-1.7
West Germany	6,715.0	6,323.9	6,916.5	-5.7	8.6	2.9
Ireland	255.2	246.2	264.4	-3.4	6.9	3.5
United Kingdom	4,155.0	4,061.3	4,329.1	-2.2	6.2	4.0
Japan	12,929.0	12,337.6	13,475.3	-4.4	8.4	4.1
Hungary	75.5	75.5	78.9	0.0	4.3	4.3
Turkey	144.2	141.3	152.3	-1.9	7.2	5.3
Canada	21,713.0	21,924.4	22,959.6	0.9	4.5	5.4
USSR	351.0	349.7	374.2	-0.3	6.5	6.2
Iceland	72.8	74.6	78.1	2.3	4.5	6.8
Sweden	849.0	856.2	912.3	0.8	6.1	6.9
Czechoslovakia	46.2	45.3	49.7	-1.8	8.9	7.0
Switzerland	856.0	889.5	921.6	3.6	3.5	7.1
France	2,245.0	2,257.4	2,428.9	0.5	7.1	7.6

(continued)

TABLE 4A.2 (continued)

Exporting Country	Exporter's F.O.B. Value ($000,000)	U.S. Import Value ($000,000)		Decomposition of C.I.F.-F.O.B. Differences (percentage points)		
		Free Alongside Ship	Cost-Insurance-Freight	Unexplained Variation	Transport Costs	Total Variation
New Zealand	350.5	347.6	385.6	-0.8	9.9	9.1
Poland	266.2	264.8	294.1	-0.5	10.0	9.5
Finland	210.1	209.4	234.2	-0.3	10.6	10.3
Denmark	450.0	471.6	503.4	4.3	6.3	10.6
Belgium	1,590.0	1,656.5	1,785.3	3.7	7.2	10.9
Australia	1,036.0	1,042.0	1,163.5	0.5	10.4	11.0
Portugal	227.4	239.4	265.5	4.5	9.8	14.4
Spain	829.0	888.4	978.9	6.1	9.2	15.3
Netherlands	1,307.4	1,432.6	1,543.4	8.1	7.2	15.3
Italy	2,300.0	2,585.0	2,832.7	10.1	8.7	18.8
Greece	122.9	157.8	174.4	20.0	9.5	29.5
South Africa	352.1	608.8	650.5	39.5	6.4	45.9
Austria	249.8	451.8	471.0	42.9	4.1	47.0
Romania	73.9	130.8	146.2	38.9	10.5	49.5
Total	60,421.1	60,642.7	64,983.9	0.3	6.7	7.0

Source: Alexander J. Yeats, "On the Accuracy of Partner Country Trade Statistics," Oxford Bulletin of Economics and Statistics 40 (November 1978):345. Reprinted by permission.

Since the relevant data are shown in Tables 4A.1 and 4A.2, correlation coefficients were run between the freight factors computed from the dual valued U.S. import statistics and the export-import f.o.b.-c.i.f. trade ratios. For the 29 developed and socialist countries shown in Table 4A.2, the correlation coefficient (r = 0.13) was far from statistically significant, while that for the 55 developing countries was actually negative (r = -0.13). Since it was felt that the latter results may have been influenced by petroleum, the oil exporting countries were dropped from the developing country group in a further test. However, the resulting correlation coefficient (r = 0.01) was positive but insignificant. Altogether, these results fail to confirm that normal f.o.b.-c.i.f. trade ratios provide a useful approximation to nominal transport and insurance costs.[*]

NOTES

1. For two views of the potential contribution of trade to growth and development, see Donald Keesing, "Outward Looking Policies and Economic Development," Economic Journal 77 (June 1967):303-20; and Gerald Meier, The International Economics of Development (New York: Harper & Row, 1968). Quantitative evidence as to the importance of tariffs and nontariff barriers as constraints to the expansion of developing country trade is presented in Alexander J. Yeats, Trade Barriers Facing Developing Countries (London: Macmillan, 1979).

2. Michael Michaely, "Exports and Growth: An Empirical Investigation," Journal of Development Economics 4 (March 1977): 49-53.

3. Benjamin Cohen, "Relative Effects of Foreign Capital and Larger Exports on Economic Development," Review of Economics and Statistics 50 (May 1968):281-84.

4. Robert Emery, "The Relation of Exports and Economic Growth," Kyklos 20 (Facs. 2, 1967):470-86. A similar approach is

---

[*]While these conclusions are based on aggregate trade data, a study shows that statistics at lower levels of aggregation may be even less reliable.[20]

employed by Joseph Haring and Joseph Humphrey, "Simple Models of Trade and Expansion," Western Economic Journal 2 (Spring 1964): 173-78.

5. Irving Kravis, "Trade as a Handmaiden of Growth: Similarities Between the Nineteenth and Twentieth Centuries," Economic Journal 80 (December 1970):850-72.

6. Ibid., p. 869.

7. J. M. Finger and A. J. Yeats, "Effective Protection by Transportation Costs and Tariffs: A Comparison of Magnitudes," Quarterly Journal of Economics 90 (February 1976):169-76.

8. Data on India's transport and insurance costs for exports to the United States were derived from U.S. Department of Commerce, U.S. General Imports: Schedule A Commodity by Country (FT 135) (Washington, D.C.: U.S. Government Printing Office, 1975). This source tabulates imports, by product by country, on a joint f.a.s. and c.i.f. basis. Taking the ratio of the c.i.f. to the f.a.s. import value provides a measure of the ad valorem incidence of international transport and insurance costs.

9. See Peter J. Lloyd, "Transport Costs on Indonesian Exports: The Australian Case," Bulletin of Indonesian Economic Studies 12 (November 1976):116-20.

10. David Brodsky and Gary Sampson, "International Transport and Latin American Exports to the United States," International Journal of Transportation Economics 7 (December 1979):279-92.

11. Carmellah Moneta, "The Estimation of Transportation Costs in International Trade, Journal of Political Economy 57 (February 1959):41-58.

12. See Alexander J. Yeats, "The Incidence of Transportation Costs on South African Exports," South African Journal of Economics 44 (Fall 1976):251; and Gary P. Sampson and Alexander J. Yeats, "Tariff and Transport Barriers Facing Australian Exports," Journal of Transport Economics and Policy 11 (May 1977).

13. UNCTAD, A Transport Strategy for Land-Locked Developing Countries (TD/B/453/Add. 1/Rev. 1) (New York: United Nations, 1974).

14. See "A Note on Tariff Valuation Bases, Economic Efficiency, and the Effects of Preferences," Journal of Political Economy 74 (August 1966):401-02; or P. A. Diamond and F. Mitchell, "Customs Valuation and Transport Choice," Journal of International Economics 1 (February 1971):119-26.

15. The selection of products was drawn from Hal Lary, Imports of Manufactures from Less Developed Countries (New York: National Bureau of Economic Research, 1968). Tariff rates were taken from the U.S. International Trade Commission, Protection in Major Trading Countries (Washington, D.C.: USITC, 1975). Since both documents classified industries and tariffs on the basis of the Standard Industrial Classification (SIC) system, the data were converted to the SITC using a cross-classification scheme developed by the U.S. State Department.

16. See Ian Little, Tibor Scitovsky, and Maurice Scott, Industry and Trade in Some Developing Countries (London: Oxford University Press, 1970).

17. Data compiled by Moneta, "Estimation of Transportation Costs," pp. 41-58, also show that developing countries pay higher transportation costs for penetration of European markets.

18. Robert Baldwin, Nontariff Distortions of International Trade (Washington, D.C.: The Brookings Institution, 1970), pp. 183-84, recommends that countries now using a c.i.f. valuation base should shift to an f.o.b. system on grounds that the latter makes more efficient use of world transportation resources.

19. For example, Oscar Morgenstern, On the Accuracy of Economic Observations (Princeton, N.J.: Princeton University Press, 1963), made basic comparisons of export-import data in an attempt to assess the underlying quality of the data. W. Beckerman, "Distance and the Pattern of Intra-European Trade," Review of Economics and Statistics, February 1956, utilized c.i.f.-f.o.b. ratios for ordinal comparisons of economic distances. Also, UNCTAD, Review of Maritime Transport, 1978-1979 (Geneva: United Nations, 1979), attempted to use f.o.b.-c.i.f. ratios to estimate the global cost of maritime transport. Numerous studies involving gravity flow trade models have also employed bilateral trade data as a basic input for approximating international freight costs.

20. See Alexander J. Yeats, "On the Accuracy of Partner Country Trade Statistics," Oxford Bulletin of Economics and Statistics, November 1978, pp. 341-61.

5

THE INFLUENCE OF
TRANSPORTATION COSTS ON
RESOURCE-BASED
INDUSTRIALIZATION
IN DEVELOPING COUNTRIES

Considering the magnitude of the debate that has appeared in the professional literature on alternative growth strategies, it is surprising that so relatively little consideration has been given to the possibility of transforming the commodity sector to serve as a catalyst to developing country industrialization. The expansion of manufactures exports from the newly industrialized countries (NICs) seemingly has diverted attention from commodities since the former have been a major concern for many developed nations. However, manufactures constitute an important part of the export base for only a few developing countries, with Hong Kong, Taiwan, and Korea having accounted for 50 percent of all such shipments in 1975, and this proportion rises to 72 percent if Mexico, Brazil, India, and Singapore are included. Given the real or imagined structural adjustment problems these few developing countries have caused for the North, there is a concern that it will be increasingly difficult to follow a similar path to industrialization and growth within the confines of existing institutional arrangements. Thus, attention is now being directed to the possible use of the commodity sector to achieve development objectives.

The interest in utilizing domestically produced commodities as a stimulus to industrialization rests in the view that increased processing is a potentially important source of domestic income, employment, or foreign exchange earnings. For example, UNCTAD has estimated that the local processing of ten selected commodities (copper, bauxite, phosphate, rubber, cotton, jute, hides and skins, nonconiferous wood, cocoa, and coffee) through the semifabricated stage would provide additional gross export earnings of about $27 billion.[1] Similar conclusions emerge from a study by R. Bosson and B. Varon that showed that if the domestic mineral production of developing countries were processed up to the metal bar stage, the annual value of this output could be $10 to $12 billion higher.[2] Related studies by Alberto Valdes and Alexander Yeats also estimate that gains of a similar order of magnitude would be associated with an expansion of processed agricultural exports.[3]

Given the dimension of the potential gains, it is of obvious importance to identify the factors that work against domestic processing in the developing countries. This chapter attempts such an evaluation with special attention given to the influence of transport costs. Since processing generally reduces bulk or stowage factors and raises product value, there is some reason to believe that freight rates should decline with increased fabrication. If such is the case then the structure of shipping costs could be a potentially important element working in favor of the location of processing activities in developing countries. However, if the actual structure of freight costs does not reflect variations in the true cost-of-carriage, then transport costs may not in fact have this beneficial effect.

THE STRUCTURE OF DEVELOPING COUNTRY EXPORTS

As an indication of the nature of developing countries' processing problems, Table 5.1 shows the components of 27 processing chains (that is, a production process in which a primary product is transformed into a semifinished good and then a finished manufacture) as well as the 1965 and 1975 proportion of OECD imports in the different stages. For the 27 processing chains combined, 58 percent of the developing countries' 1975 exports consisted of unprocessed commodities while only 22 percent were fully processed products. In contrast, raw form commodities accounted for only 39 percent of total OECD imports while processed products comprised 33 percent. Thus imports from developing countries are much more concentrated on unprocessed products than those from other nations.

While the data show variation on an individual product basis, a clear tendency exists for developing country exports to be concentrated on the raw form products across processing chains. Specifically, in only one-third of the 27 commodity chains did the proportion of semifinished and finished goods exceed 50 percent. A further point to be noted concerning the disproportionate share of developing country exports in the raw form is that only in the case of meat, groundnuts, and leather was the unprocessed portion of developing countries' exports lower than that for other suppliers.

Table 5.1 seemingly suggests that developing countries made some general progress over 1965-75 toward more highly processed exports. Raw form commodities, which represented 74 percent of total exports in 1965, accounted for only 58 percent in 1975. The decline in the raw form proportion was mainly due to the final processing stage where exports rose from 8 percent (with a value of

$1.2 million) to 22 percent of the total in 1975 (with a value of $9.1 million). However, this improvement was concentrated in a few commodities, over half of it being attributable to cotton clothing ($4.5 billion) and leather goods ($1.2 billion). At the semiprocessed stage, improvements were largely confined to refined sugar, simply worked wood, and unwrought copper. From the viewpoint of this chapter, a key question concerns the influence of transport costs on these changes in the structure of developing country trade.

Any integrated assessment of the influence of transport costs on developing country processing problems must also consider the effects of other factors that stimulate or retard this activity. A major positive element is that, as owners of the natural resource or primary product, the developing countries have some control over its disposition. However, there are a number of other factors pertaining to tariffs and nontariff barriers, market structure, technology, and finance that seemingly have negative effects.

Tariffs and Nontariff Barriers

Numerous studies have noted that industrial country tariffs generally increase or escalate as one moves from exports of unprocessed commodities to semifinished goods or manufactures. It has been argued[4] that such a system maintains developing countries as raw material exporters since they are unable to overcome the higher import duties applied to processed goods.* Therefore, a key question concerns the potential influence of tariffs and other artificial trade restraints on the structure of imports from developing countries.

Several empirical studies clearly reveal the restrictiveness of trade barriers facing <u>processed</u> commodities, particularly those in the agricultural sector. As one example, Odd Gulbrandsen and Assar Lindbeck concluded that "an intricate system of tariffs,

---

*It should be noted that escalating tariff structures are not a <u>necessary</u> condition for establishing a bias against processed good exports since the restrictive effect of the import duty will be influenced by the elasticity of import demand for individual products. Since most empirical studies show that these elasticities rise with fabrication, a constant nominal tariff will have more of a retardation effect on processed goods than on primary forms of the commodity.

TABLE 5.1

Percentage Distribution of OECD Imports by Stage of Processing in 1965 and 1975

Processing Chain and Components	Raw Form				Semiprocessed Form				Processed Form			
	Developing Countries		Total		Developing Countries		Total		Developing Countries		Total	
	1965	1975	1965	1975	1965	1975	1965	1975	1965	1975	1965	1975
Coffee[a]												
Coffee beans, coffee extracts	99	95	98	93	—	—	—	—	0.3	5	2	7
Cocoa												
Cocoa beans, powder and butter, chocolate	90	78	62	50	10	21	19	25	0.2	1	19	25
Sugar												
Raw, refined, sugar preparations	98	66	83	54	2	34	11	40	0.2	0.5	6	6
Rubber[a]												
Natural rubber, rubber products	99	92	59	25	—	—	—	—	1	8	41	75
Cotton												
Raw cotton, yarns and fabric, clothing	59	17	35	13	14	11	21	17	27	72	44	70
Jute												
Raw jute, fabrics, jute sacks	38	18	35	16	55	62	54	57	7	20	11	27

Commodity												
Sisal[a]												
Fibers, cordage	83	65	53	29	—	—	—	—	17	35	47	71
Copper												
Ores, unwrought, wrought	10	21	8	19	86	78	75	59	4	1	18	22
Tin												
Ores, unwrought, wrought	33	21	26	18	67	79	73	81	0	0.1	0.6	2
Meat[a]												
Fresh and frozen, prepared	76	68	79	83	—	—	—	—	24	32	21	17
Groundnuts[a]												
Groundnuts, groudnut oil	77	52	77	60	—	—	—	—	23	48	23	40
Copra[a]												
Copra, coconut oil	75	48	69	44	—	—	—	—	25	52	31	56
Palm kernel[a]												
Palm kernel, palm kernel oil	90	35	79	31	—	—	—	—	10	65	21	69
Wood												
Rough wood, plywood, manufactures	63	53	25	34	36	40	68	55	0.6	8	7	11
Iron												
Ores, pig iron/ingots, manufactures	93	82	42	36	7	18	54	60	0	0.2	4	5
Phosphates												
Phosphate rock, acids, superphosphate	91	85	66	80	4	4	18	9	5	11	16	11

(continued)

TABLE 5.1 (continued)

Processing Chain and Components	Raw Form				Semiprocessed Form				Processed Form			
	Developing Countries		Total		Developing Countries		Total		Developing Countries		Total	
	1965	1975	1965	1975	1965	1975	1965	1975	1965	1975	1965	1975
Manganese[a]												
Ores, ferro manganese	93	94	68	60	—	—	—	65	7	6	31	40
Aluminum[b]												
Bauxite, unwrought, wrought	81	35	18	11	17	63	63	65	2	2	20	23
Fish[a]												
Fresh and frozen, preparations	77	86	71	80	—	—	—	—	23	14	29	20
Fruit[a]												
Fresh fruit, preserved fruit	86	81	80	77	—	—	—	—	14	19	20	23
Vegetables[a]												
Fresh vegetables, preserved vegetables	78	72	80	72	—	—	—	—	22	28	20	29

Tobacco											
Unmanufactured, manufactured — 96	95	88	75	—	—	—	—	4	5	12	25
Leather											
Hides, leather, leather goods — 49	12	35	15	30	20	23	17	22	68	42	69
Pulp and Paper											
Pulp wood, paper pulp, paper products — 20	5	3	3	47	47	37	33	33	49	60	63
Wool											
Raw wool, yarn, wool fabrics — 95	89	61	50	1	8	15	18	4	14	25	32
Lead											
Ores, unwrought, wrought lead — 40	51	31	33	59	48	67	64	1	1	2	3
Zinc											
Ores, unwrought, wrought zinc — 72	74	46	49	26	25	50	47	2	1	4	4

[a] No intermediate stage could be identified from trade data for the processing chain.

[b] Alumina (SITC 513.6) is included in the intermediate stage.

Source: Adapted from UNCTAD, The Processing Before Export of Primary Commodities: Areas for Further International Co-operation (Manila: UNCTAD, May 1979).

nontariff barriers, and subsidies result in an average level of agricultural protectionism of almost 70 percent for the European Community, 80 percent in Sweden, 102 percent in Norway, and 103 percent in Switzerland."[5] This study also demonstrated that the level of agricultural protectionism in industrial countries averaged over three times that for manufactures in the 1970s, and that both the level and coverage of this protection have been rapidly increasing.

The magnitude of the trade barriers facing selected processed agricultural products is illustrated in Table 5.2. Shown here are nominal and effective tariff rates, as well as total effective protection from tariffs and nontariff barriers in the EEC, Japan, Norway, Sweden, and the United States. As indicated, the rate of effective protection is several times the nominal rate, but the divergence is particularly high for vegetable oils and dairy products. However, the remarkable fact that emerges from Table 5.2 concerns the magnitude of the trade barriers facing these agricultural products. While the average effective rate of protection for manufactures has been estimated at about 20 percent in industrial countries, rates of several hundred percent are observed for some agricultural products.

Aside from processed agricultural goods, evidence suggests that markets for processed fibers may be even more restricted by tariffs and nontariff barriers. Some indication of the influence of these restrictions on developing country exports can be derived from a passage in the World Development Report:

> The provisions of the Multi-Fibre Arrangement designed
> to protect exporters have been weakened, and in the past
> year more restrictive quotas have been imposed. The
> new quotas in the European Common Market, for instance,
> do not merely limit growth but actually reduce import
> levels (author's emphasis). For three leading suppliers
> (the Republic of China, Hong Kong and the Republic of
> Korea) quotas for 1978 are well below their actual 1976
> trade levels in several major product categories. All
> the significant and potentially significant exporters have
> seen their scope for expanding exports severely restric-
> ted by quotas that grow only slowly from past trade lev-
> els, usually by between 0.5 percent and 4 percent a
> year, compared with the previous norm of 6 percent a
> year. The new agreements also establish low "trigger
> levels" for further quotas that limit the scope for diver-
> sification of exports into new products. Restrictive new
> quotas have been imposed by other importing countries
> such as Australia, Canada, Norway and Sweden, while

TABLE 5.2

Comparison of Nominal and Effective Rates of Protection for Processed Agricultural Products in the European Economic Community, Japan, Norway, Sweden, and the United States
(all figures in percent)

Product Name	European Economic Community			Japan		Norway		Sweden			United States	
	Tariff Rate		Effective Protection[a]	Nominal Protection	Effective Protection[b]	Nominal Protection	Effective Protection[b]	Tariff Rate		Effective Protection[a]	Nominal Protection	Effective Protection[b]
	Nominal	Effective						Nominal	Effective			
Meat products	19.5	36.6	165.0 (90)[c]	17.9	69.1	21.6	75.2 (50)	0.0	0.0	0.0	5.9	10.3 (5)
Preserved sea foods	21.5	52.6	52.6 (50)	13.6	34.7	5.4	14.4	4.1	11.6	9.3	6.0	15.6 (20)
Preserved fruit and vegetables	20.5	44.9	74.7	18.5	49.3	31.1	99.8 (80)	13.4	40.1	34.8	14.8	36.8 (35)
Dairy products												
Cheese	23.0	58.8	276.0 (180)	35.3	174.7	11.4	54.8 (70)	0.0	0.0	178.3 (100)	11.5	34.5 (50)
Butter	21.0	76.5	1327.7 (90)	45.0	417.7	91.2	879.4 (700)	0.0	0.0	1157.6 (1000)	10.3	46.7 (70)
Condensed and evaporated milk	21.3	44.3	334.4 (400)	31.7	153.9	41.2	208.2 (120)	0.0	0.0	56.3 (200)	10.7	29.6 (50)
Grain and grain products												
Corn milling	12.0	21.8	82.1	25.6	68.7	0.1	0.0	0.0	0.0	165.3	4.3	0.0 (15)
Rice milling	16.0	70.3	105.9	15.0	49.0	3.0	3.8	0.0	0.0	0.0	36.2	327.6 (320)
Prepared foods	5.6	0.0	-50.0 (-20)	0.7	-21.2	0.3	0.0 (10)	0.0	0.0	-70.1	6.2	7.4 (0)
Flour and cereal preparations	20.1	48.9	94.7	23.8	75.4	2.2	5.6 (10)	2.9	13.7	101.7	10.9	34.8 (70)
Bakery products	12.0	0.9	0.0	20.9	17.3	21.3	42.4 (30)	16.5	36.0	13.9	1.9	0.0 (-10)
Prepared and processed food												
Pickles and dressings	20.1	25.9	25.9	21.9	59.8	44.7	248.7	8.9	38.8	38.8	9.4	-26.9 (-20)
Roasted coffee	15.2	35.7	35.7	35.0	137.1	4.4	13.8	0.0	0.6	0.6	0.0	0.0
Cocoa powder and butter	13.6	76.0	76.0	15.0	125.0	3.7	30.7	2.0	16.8	16.8	2.6	22.0
Misc. food products	12.0	6.7	6.7	28.6	58.2	14.3	40.1	54.8	175.2	175.2	2.7	0.2 (5)
Vegetable oils												
Coconut oil	11.5	132.9	132.9	9.0	49.2	5.8	30.0	0.0	0.0	1049.9	9.4	16.3
Cottonseed oil	11.0	79.0	79.0	25.8	200.3	4.6	34.0	0.0	0.0	486.0	59.6	465.9
Groundnut oil	11.3	139.7	139.7	14.2	96.5	5.3	28.7	0.0	0.0	879.4	15.0	6.7
Soyabean oil	11.0	148.1	148.1	25.4	268.3	8.0	110.7	0.0	0.0	1478.3	22.5	252.9
Rapeseed oil	9.0	57.2	57.2	15.1	22.3	6.0	36.2	0.0	0.0	617.5	20.8	60.9
Palm kernel oil	10.5	141.5	141.5	7.2	49.2	2.1	9.5	0.0	0.0	82.9	3.8	29.2

[a] Includes levies and other special charges.

[b] Effective tariff protection.

[c] Data in parentheses include other nontariff barriers.

Source: Alexander J. Yeats, "Effective Protection for Processed Agricultural Products: A Comparison of Industrial Countries," Journal of Economics and Business, Fall 1976, Table 1, p. 35. Reprinted by permission.

the United States, in its new bilateral agreements, has
held the quotas of its largest suppliers at the same level
in 1978 as in 1977. Although the growth of imports has
been greater than the limits established in the past, and
this divergence may also occur in future years, the recent measures are more restrictive than previous ones
and will reduce the growth in textile and clothing exports.
They will affect exports not only from the major exporters
but also from the smaller, poorer, and less advanced
developing countries where textile products usually make
up a large share of manufactured exports.[6]

Aside from textiles and agriculture, tariffs and nontariff restraints tend to be a problem of varying degrees in other commodity
sectors. However, it is generally conceded that these restrictions
are applied most often and have their most important effects on the
types of labor-intensive processed commodities in which developing
countries are generally acknowledged to have an important comparative advantage in production.

Market Structure Barriers

While tariffs and nontariff barriers are important trade barriers, an impediment to further processing often is the market power
of foreign firms. For example, international comparisons of production and sales data show that tightly controlled oligopolistic market
structures exist for processed commodities like rubber (tires), coffee, cocoa, bauxite, and zinc. As such, consideration must be given
to how developing countries can compete with the entrenched firms.

An UNCTAD study of cocoa processing problems indicates
the potential importance of market structure barriers. The report
specifically notes that

nine companies account for 80 percent of the total production of chocolate and other cocoa products in the U.S.
and Western Europe and competition takes the form
mainly of product differentiation. Different brand names
facilitate product selection by the consumer, and help in
preserving the market for particular product lines. Advertising is a major activity directed toward this end,
the scale of advertising expenditures by chocolate manufacturing firms providing a good indicator of the effort
made to exploit product differentiation. Since advertising
expenditures appear to be increasingly concentrated

among the largest companies, this element also contributes to the further concentration of sales among these companies.[7]

The UNCTAD report also notes that

the close link between success in selling particular lines of chocolate and an inevitably costly advertising campaign constitutes a financial barrier for new firms. Usually, the required advertising cost can be supported only by a large company with substantial financial resources. This entry barrier represents a major obstacle to the manufacture of chocolate for export by developing countries.

Aside from cocoa, these observations raise important questions concerning the likely success of developing country efforts to move into processed commodity markets. For example, in coffee, tobacco, rubber, or various metals sectors it may be impractical to consider "toehold" entry since competitive factors may dictate entry in considerable scale (possibly through acquisition of an established firm) with a sizavle advertising budget.

This relation between market structure and developing country export penetration can be illustrated graphically. First, statistics on the percentage of U.S. domestic sales controlled by the largest four firms were drawn from a selection of 100 industries from U.S. Census Department data.* Next, existing concordances were employed to match these sales data (which were on the SIC system) to the SITC. UN trade data were then used to compute the developing country share of imports for each industry. Figure 5.1 shows the scatter diagram for these developing country market shares against the four firm concentration ratios, as well as a plot of the least squares regression (LL) fitted to these data. The results are

---

*In the selection an attempt was made to exclude industries that had a large-scale expansion of operations into developing countries. Here, it was hypothesized, the normal market structure relation need not hold since imports could enter the United States under the protective umbrella of parent companies. It should be noted, however, that such associations may not be in the developing countries' interest given the transnationals' practices like transfer pricing.

FIGURE 5.1

The Relation between Market Structure and the Share of
Developing Countries in U.S. Imports:
Selected Manufacturing Industries

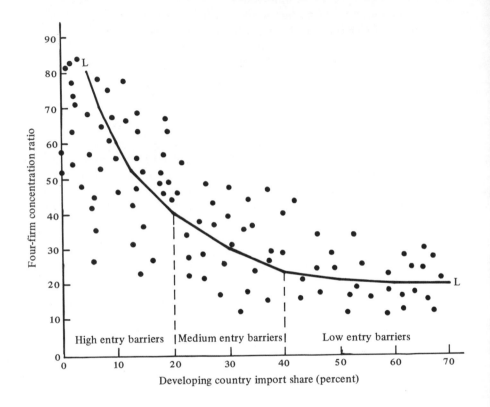

Source: Constructed by the author.

significant at the 99 percent level, and an R^2 of over 50 percent tes-
tifies to the close association that exists between the variables.

While further research is needed, the position of LL and the
scatter diagram suggest several important points. First, it appears
that three stages exist in the normal market structure-export penetration relation. Where four-firm concentration ratios exceed 40
percent, developing countries appear to have great difficulty in coun-
tering the market power of established concerns. This is shown by
the fact that the curve LL becomes almost vertical above this point,

and the developing countries are normally able to achieve positions only as marginal suppliers, generally contributing 20 percent of the market or less. Thus, markets with concentration ratios of 40 percent or more should probably be thought of as having high entry barriers, and as being very difficult for developing country penetration. Between 20 and 40 percent concentration ratios, an interval defined as having moderate entry barriers, the developing country import share may normally vary between 20 and 50 percent. Market structure is undoubtedly a factor, but it seems that other influences like tariffs or nontariff barriers may assume equal importance. At concentration ratios of less than 20 percent, easy entry seemingly exists with market structure playing a minor role in influencing import shares.*

Transfer of Technology

Restrictions on the transfer of technology may be another obstacle to industrialization through domestic processing. In minerals and metals, as well as some food processing industries, patents, technologies, and licenses are often owned by transnational corporations and conditions concerning their transfer may preclude adoption by developing countries. For example, one restrictive practice often imposed is limitations on exports produced with the imported technology. This restriction may be exercised through contractual arrangements requiring prior approval for the supply or pricing of exports. A further problem may arise when a technology is transferred from a transnational solely to a developing country subsidiary. In such a case, the benefits of the transfer are restricted to the associate and are not available to other firms.

---

*The nature of the causal factors operating behind this relation should be clearly set forth. Penetration of highly concentrated markets calls for the ability to mobilize financial and other productive resources on a considerable scale for effective competition with entrenched firms. The developing country share of imports is consistently lower since these nations often do not have the required resources for market penetration. Returning to the example of chocolate, high advertising expenditures may not be an insurmountable barrier for Swiss firms exporting chocolate to the U.S. market, but they may be prohibitive for developing countries.

Control of technology is further strengthened by the possession of technical expertise. Even when technology is made freely available, its implementation and maintenance often require skilled manpower not always available locally. Thus, whether this technical expertise is formally tied to technology provided by a transnational corporation, or is simply not available locally, it can be an important factor restricting the competitiveness of developing countries aiming to establish local processing facilities.

The transnational corporation's control over production inputs and outputs may be another obstacle to the establishment of new processing plants in developing countries. This control may take the form of irregular or short supplies, or higher prices for inputs while maintaining pegged transfer prices for outputs. In such cases, a new entrant must secure some control over production inputs in order not to be subject to adverse pressures and practices of established firms.

While it is far beyond this chapter's scope to fully examine ways in which technology problems and restrictive business practices inhibit developing country processing of raw materials, the importance of this factor should not be underestimated.[8] Certainly liberalization in constraints to technological transfer will have to occur if this factor is not to remain an important barrier to resource-based industrialization.

Financial Constraints

The magnitude of the capital investment required to establish local processing often is another obstacle facing developing countries. As an illustration, Table 5.3 shows that average mid-1970 investment costs for mineral and metal processing plants ranged from $80 million for a zinc smelting plant capable of producing 50,000 tons a year to $1.2 billion for a 500,000-ton aluminum plant. Imposing as these figures are, they do not include required investments in infrastructure, such as transport facilities, or incorporate the effects of recent inflation.

While investment costs for processing agricultural products are of a lower order of magnitude, they are still sufficient to pose a major problem for many developing countries. For example, the Tropical Products Institute estimates that $700,000 is required to construct a soluble coffee plant for processing 17,000 bags of coffee. Another study prepared for UNCTAD shows a cocoa roasting and grinding plant requires investments of about $12 million, while a cocoa butter and powder plant costs between $1 and $3 million. A relatively small rubber tire plant requires investments of $10 million, and a medium-sized plant would cost twice this amount.

TABLE 5.3

Estimated Average Investment Costs for Metal Processing Plants
in the Mid-1970s

Commodity	Optimum Capacity (tons per year)	1975 Investment Cost ($ million)
Aluminum	500,000	1,200
Copper	100,000	600
Iron-ore pellets	10,000,000	800
Nickel	30,000	480
Lead	100,000	140
Zinc	50,000	80

Source: UNCTAD, The Processing Before Export of Primary
Commodities: Areas for Further International Co-operation (Manila:
UNCTAD, May 1979), p. 30.

Machinery for a mill processing between 20,000 and 30,000 tons of
sisal costs about $4.1 million, while required equipment for a jute
mill entails an investment of about $11 million. Capital costs for cot-
ton processing plants range between $60 and $90 million. Again it
must be noted that all these figures need to be adjusted upward due to
existing inflation rates.

The magnitude of plant and required infrastructure investments
could therefore be a major obstacle to the expansion of processing in
developing countries, particularly for metals. However, for proper
assessment these investment costs should be contrasted with the
amount of international financing available to developing countries for
such activity. Unfortunately, a recent UNCTAD study has demonstrated just how deficient these funds have been in relation to investment needs.[9]

Among other findings, the UNCTAD study showed that the
World Bank and the International Development Agency have allocated
less than $3.3 million to developing country processing activities.
This amount, roughly equivalent to three aluminum processing plants,
illustrates the dilemma developing countries face. Stated simply,
there is no international agency now providing the financing required

for large-scale domestic processing so there is often no alternative for such funds except transnational corporations.

TRANSPORT COSTS AND COMMODITY PROCESSING

While the preceding analysis indicates there are a variety of factors that work against domestic processing in developing countries, there is some reason to suggest that transport costs may serve to encourage this activity. Specifically, processing generally lowers bulk or stowage factors while product value increases. This should work toward lower ad valorem freight costs for the processed good. However, it must be recognized that the processing function can render goods more fragile, difficult to handle, or subject to pilferage. All of these factors could lead to higher freight costs. It has also been shown that liner conference freight rates are administered prices that often discriminate against weaker elements. If these charges are in fact levied on an other than cost basis it could be another reason why actual freight rates fail to behave in the anticipated manner.

Since much detailed information concerning international transport costs has recently become available, the incidence and structure of these charges need not be left entirely to conjecture. Specifically, Chapter 2 noted that U.S. import statistics now provide information on international freight costs at very low levels of product detail. Analysis of the behavior of these charges within a processing-chain framework can provide much useful information concerning the influence of international transportation costs on the location of processing industries.

Several studies have used these data to analyze the behavior of freight costs over processing chains. For example, Table 5.4 shows the incidence of international transport costs for Indian exports of items that clearly formed part of a commodity processing chain. Where possible, the table also shows the incidence of transport costs on similar exports from another Asian country so these data could be compared with the Indian experience. However, in making these latter comparisons, the available data were quite limited since so few other Asian nations exported all stages of the processing chains to the United States.

Examination of the data in Table 5.4 indicates that the ad valorem rates for international transport costs do not behave in the anticipated manner, at least so far as the Indian export experience is concerned. For 10 of these 14 processing chains, the nominal shipping rates actually increase, often by a very considerable margin, while in two of the cases (cotton products and metal manufactures) the rates remain essentially unchanged. Among the largest increases in nominal transport rates are those recorded for tobacco, wood products, paper, and rubber—each up by 20 percentage points or more—while leather experiences a rise of over 10 percentage points. Only in the case of textile products, which are of special interest to India, do the rates remain steady or decrease. The nominal transport factor for cotton clothing declines two percentage points below that for raw cotton, while jute fabrics have a rate of 16 percentage points lower than that for raw jute. However, offsetting these declines is a rise of five percentage points in the freight factor for wool products.

Table 5.5 presents similar information on the structure of transport costs facing South African exporters of commodities at different levels of fabrication. These data also show the general perverse tendency for ad valorem freight rates to increase with processing. For 10 of the 12 processing chains that could be identified in the South African export data, the nominal transport costs increase and often by a large margin. For example, the ad valorem transport rate for leather manufactures (14.6 percent) is more than three times the nominal rate for hides and skins. Ad valorem shipping rates for wool, paper, fish, clothing, and copper are all twice as high in the final stage of processing as for the primary input. Only in the case of vegetable oils and iron and steel products do the nominal transport costs decline with fabrication. As such, Table 5.5 shows that the structure of freight rates facing South African exporters may have an important retardation effect on the growth of many processing industries.

Freight Cost Structure: A General Analysis

A key question concerns the extent to which the Indian and South African findings hold for other countries. In search of an answer, the U.S. statistics were employed for a comprehensive assessment of the relation between nominal freight costs and the level of commodity processing.

Before proceeding, it must be noted that difficulties exist in such an effort to evaluate the transport cost profile of imports composing a processing chain. While tariffs are determined in national schedules and, apart from preferential trading arrangements, apply to all exporters, transport costs may vary due to various factors. For example, nominal freight rates depend both on the price of the exported product as well as international shipping charges. Both measures may be unstable in the short run and sensitive to changes in supply or demand. Apart from these factors, distance also affects

TABLE 5.4

Analysis of the Ad Valorem Incidence of International Transportation Costs on Indian Exports to the United States, by Stage of Processing
(all figures in percent)

SITC Groups	Description	Exporters	Transportation Factors		
			Primary Product	Intermediate Goods	Product
242-251-641	Wood in the rough, paper pulp, paper and board	India	13.1	24.8	40.0
		Philippines	22.1	n.a.	37.2
262-651[a]-653[a]	Raw wool, wool yarn, wool fabrics[b]	India	9.5	18.5	14.8
263-651[a]-841[a]	Raw cotton, textile yarn, cotton clothing	India	17.8	26.9	15.9
		Hong Kong	21.8	10.9	7.5
264-651[a]-653[a]	Raw jute, jute yarn, jute fabric	India	36.0	27.5	20.0
		Bangladesh	34.3	34.5	19.3
671-673-674	Pig iron, iron and steel bars, iron plates	India	17.0	20.1	46.9
		Taiwan	11.8	9.7	11.9
671-679-698	Pig iron, iron castings, metal manufactures	India	17.1	28.5	16.8
		Korea	8.3	10.7	12.9

SITC	Description	Country			
051[a]–053	Fresh nuts, prepared nuts	India	6.3	—	24.8
		Taiwan	3.6	—	13.2
		Hong Kong	8.9	—	11.6
054–055[a]	Fresh vegetables, prepared vegetables	India	15.9	—	23.4
		Philippines	15.9	—	16.5
061–062	Sugar and honey, sugar confectionary	India	9.3	—	20.5
		Philippines	8.4	—	18.2
121–122	Unmanufactured tobacco, tobacco manufactures	India	47.4	—	70.3
		Philippines	17.1	—	9.7
211–611–612	Hides and skins, leather, leather manufactures	India	8.5	9.4	21.1
		Japan	5.7	5.3	6.8
221–422	Oil seeds and nuts, fixed vegetable oils	India	14.5	—	10.4
		Japan	10.2	—	8.6
231–629	Crude rubber, articles of rubber	India	9.6	—	35.0
		Malaysia	8.9	—	23.3
242–243–631	Wood in the rough, wood shaped, plywood	India	13.1	16.1	34.9
		Malaysia	n.a.	32.2	23.3
		Philippines	22.1	n.a.	37.9

[a] Denotes a transportation factor computed for part of the SITC group.

[b] Transport cost information for another Asian country was not available for the full processing chain.

Source: Alexander J. Yeats, "A Comparative Analysis of Tariffs and Transportation Costs on India's Exports," Journal of Development Studies 14 (October 1977):103. Reprinted by permission of Frank Cass & Co. Ltd., London.

TABLE 5.5

Ad Valorem Transport Costs and MFN Tariffs Borne by South African Exports to the United States

Processing Chain	Estimated Ad Valorem Rate (percent)		
	Transport	MFN Tariffs	Total
Leather			
Hides and skins (211)*	4.3	0.1	4.4
Leather (611)	3.9	4.8	8.7
Leather manufactures (612)	14.6	5.0	19.6
Wool			
Raw wool (262)	6.3	16.9	23.2
Wool fabrics (653)	15.1	19.2	34.3
Articles of wool (656)	12.2	18.4	30.6
Vegetable oil			
Oilseeds (221)	37.6	10.7	48.3
Fixed vegetable oils (422)	4.4	7.2	11.6
Paper			
Paper pulp (251)	14.4	0.0	14.4
Paper and board (641)	69.7	3.0	72.7
Paper articles (642)	34.8	7.2	42.0
Wood			
Rough wood (242)	29.6	0.0	29.6
Shaped wood (243)	23.9	0.0	23.9
Wood manufactures (632)	48.6	5.7	54.3
Fish			
Fresh fish (031)	6.4	0.5	6.9
Preserved fish (032)	20.0	4.7	24.7
Cotton			
Textile yarn (651)	12.3	14.8	27.1
Cotton fabrics (652)	13.9	21.1	35.0
Clothing (841)	28.4	22.1	50.5
Iron			
Ingots (672)	47.2	7.4	54.6
Iron bars (673)	24.6	5.7	30.3
Iron sheets (674)	23.5	8.3	31.8
Iron forgings (679)	17.7	8.1	25.8
Metal manufactures (698)	23.8	8.1	31.9

TABLE 5.5 (continued)

| Processing Chain | Estimated Ad Valorem Rate (percent) | | |
	Transport	MFN Tariffs	Total
Copper			
Unwrought copper (682.1)	2.4	1.7	4.1
Copper rods (682.21)	5.5	4.5	10.0
Copper tubes (682.26)	8.3	8.3	16.6
Zinc			
Unwrought zinc (686.1)	4.7	4.8	9.5
Zinc plates (686.2)	6.7	6.8	13.5
Nickel			
Unwrought nickel (683.1)	4.0	0.0	4.0
Nickel powders (683.2)	6.5	5.2	11.7
Average of above			
Primary stage	15.6	5.4	21.0
Final manufacture	19.3	8.9	28.2

*U.S. Schedule A classification numbers are shown in parentheses. This classification scheme is equivalent to the SITC system through the three-digit level, while a close correspondence exists through five-digit data.

Source: Alexander J. Yeats, "The Incidence of Transport Costs on South African Exports," South African Journal of Economics 44 (Fall 1976):249. Reprinted by permission.

the transport profile of different commodities and countries. For example, a nation that is far removed from an export market should, ceteris paribus, experience higher transport costs than one enjoying a more favorable location. As such, simply calculating the average ad valorem transportation rate for U.S. imports of products at different processing stages may not yield a reasonable approximation to the experience of individual countries.

To rectify this potential problem a two-stage approach was used. First, overall ad valorem freight rates were calculated for all U.S. imports comprising different stages of fabrication irrespective of the countries of origin. This procedure permitted an evaluation of the way in which transport costs influence the competitive position of processing industries in the United States. Next, similar ratios were derived (where possible) for specific countries in order to evaluate the behavior of freight charges when the mix of exporting nations is held constant. Analysis of these data should indicate the extent to which the structure of ocean freight rates stimulates, or retards, the growth of processing industries in primary-product-producing nations.

Table 5.6 presents nominal transportation and insurance costs for products forming successive links in a processing chain. The table shows the U.S. post-Tokyo Round tariffs, and also gives the freight factor for each product. To assist in evaluating the joint influence of transport and tariff charges at each level of fabrication, their combined ad valorem rate is given.

The impression that emerges from Table 5.6 is that the tendency for transport costs to decline with increased processing is not as important as some economists suggest. While 13 of the 21 processed products register lower ad valorem freight rates than those for the primary stage, in two cases—fish and copper—the reduction is limited to about 1 percentage point. However, there are items where the processed product clearly does enter the United States under lower shipping charges. Groundnut and palm-kernel oil, jute, iron, and aluminum all experience freight rate declines ranging from 10 to over 20 percentage points. In these instances, the fall in nominal shipping costs is more than sufficient to offset the escalated structure of MFN tariffs. However, in other cases—preserved vegetables, leather, rubber, wood, and cotton—it appears that transportation costs increase and reinforce the tendency of the tariff structure to protect domestic U.S. processing industries.*

---

*While the results must be evaluated on a product-by-product basis, certain increases in nominal shipping rates should not be altogether unexpected. The rise in freight costs for plywood may be due to problems in handling this relatively (to bulk lumber) fragile item. Similarly, higher stevedoring costs, as well as increased insurance charges to protect against damage or pilferage, may be a factor for processed wood, cotton, and leather products. Relatively high ratios for the volumes of primary to processed good shipments could be another reason for the rising freight costs if there are important economies of scale in transport.

While the freight rates shown in Table 5.6 reflect the influence of international transportation costs on the competition position of U.S. processing industries, they may not be representative of the rate profile of individual nations if the mix of exporting countries changes at different levels of fabrication. To evaluate the actual experience of specific primary-product-producing countries, an analysis of U.S. import statistics was conducted with the objective of identifying those nations that exported each stage of processing for the products shown in Table 5.6. Estimation of the ad valorem transport costs for these specific countries will show how transport costs actually vary with increased fabrication as opposed to the extent to which the apparent change (Table 5.6) in freight rates is due to shifting sources of supply.

Table 5.7 presents information on the ad valorem incidence of shipping costs for primary and processed goods exported by specific developing countries. Since it was not possible to identify nations that exported all stages of the items under study, the analysis was confined to the 14 processing chains for which such information was available. Also, for some of the metals (copper, aluminum, lead) only one or two developing countries exported both the primary and processed forms of the product to the United States. In these instances, the specific country analysis was limited. However, in the case of certain other items—leather, vegetables, or fish—the number of exporting developing countries was sufficiently large to necessitate the use of a sample for each item.

The data shown in Table 5.7 indicate that the average freight factors for U.S. imports understate the transport cost profiles facing some developing countries. For example, the average ad valorem freight rate for U.S. imports (all sources) of natural rubber is approximately 10 percent, while this factor rises to over 15 percent for rubber manufactures. However, this increase has been moderated considerably by shifts in the source of supply from developing countries for the primary good to industrial nations for imports of rubber manufactures.* When nominal transport costs for processed rubber goods are computed for those countries that are primary product producers (that is, Brazil, India, Malaysia), the average freight

---

*For example, in 1973 the United States imported over $400 million worth of crude rubber (SITC 231) with approximately 85 percent of this total originating in developing countries. However, for imports of rubber manufactures (SITC 621), the developing country share was under 5 percent of the total.

TABLE 5.6

Estimated Ad Valorem Tariff and Transport Costs for Exports to the United States, by Stage of Processing

Processing Chain		Processing Stage				Percentage Point Change
		Primary Product	I	II	Final Good	
Meat products						
Fresh meat (011), meat preparations (013)	Tariffs	4.6	—	—	4.7	0.1
	Transport	10.1	—	—	4.9	-5.2
	Total	14.7	—	—	9.6	-5.1
Fish						
Fresh fish (031), fish preparations (032)	Tariffs	1.3	—	—	9.8	8.5
	Transport	6.8	—	—	5.6	-1.2
	Total	8.1	—	—	15.4	7.3
Fruit						
Fresh fruit (051), fruit preparations (053)	Tariffs	5.6	—	—	5.0	-0.6
	Transport	27.2	—	—	11.5	-15.7
	Total	32.8	—	—	16.5	-16.3
Vegetables						
Fresh vegetables (054), pre-served vegetables	Tariffs	8.9	—	—	8.0	-0.9
	Transport	4.3	—	—	14.9	10.6
	Total	13.2	—	—	22.9	9.7

Cocoa						
Cocoa beans (072.1), powder and butter (072.2, 072.3), chocolate	Tariffs	0.0	1.6	—	4.8	4.8
	Transport	5.0	6.5	—	8.1	3.1
	Total	5.0	8.1	—	12.9	7.9
Leather						
Hides (211), leather (611), leather goods (612), shoes (851)	Tariffs	1.1	4.7	7.7	14.0	12.9
	Transport	3.9	4.5	6.2	9.1	5.2
	Total	5.0	9.2	13.9	23.1	18.1
Groundnuts						
Groundnuts (221.1), groundnut oil (ex. 421.4)	Tariffs	25.7	—	—	24.1	-1.6
	Transport	14.7	—	—	2.9	-11.8
	Total	40.4	—	—	27.0	-13.4
Copra						
Copra (221.2), coconut oil (ex. 422.3)	Tariffs	0.0	—	—	5.5	5.5
	Transport	6.2	—	—	2.7	-3.5
	Total	6.2	—	—	8.2	2.0
Palm kernel						
Palm kernels (221.3), palm kernel oil (ex. 422.4)	Tariffs	0.0	—	—	3.2	3.2
	Transport	25.0	—	—	4.9	-20.1
	Total	25.0	—	—	8.1	-16.9
Rubber						
Natural rubber (231.1), rubber goods (629)	Tariffs	0.0	—	—	4.6	4.6
	Transport	9.9	—	—	15.6	5.7
	Total	9.9	—	—	20.2	10.3

(continued)

TABLE 5.6 (continued)

Processing Chain		Primary Product	Processing Stage I	II	Final Good	Percentage Point Change
Wood						
Rough wood (242.2), simply worked wood (243), plywood (631.2), wood manufactures (632)	Tariffs	0.0	0.3	8.5	6.7	6.7
	Transport	2.9	7.0	17.2	8.6	5.7
	Total	2.9	7.3	25.7	15.3	12.4
Paper						
Pulpwood (241.1), wood pulp (251), paper and articles (ex. 64)	Tariffs	0.0	0.0	—	2.5	2.5
	Transport	7.0	0.9	—	3.5	-3.5
	Total	7.0	0.9	—	6.0	-1.0
Wool						
Raw wool (262.1), wool yarn (651.2), fabrics (653.2), clothing (ex. 841.1)	Tariffs	9.7	20.7	20.7	16.6	6.9
	Transport	8.9	12.7	5.0	9.6	0.7
	Total	18.6	33.4	25.7	26.2	7.6
Cotton						
Raw cotton (263.1), cotton yarn (651.3), fabrics (652), clothing (ex. 841.1)	Tariffs	6.2	10.5	13.8	20.0	13.8
	Transport	4.3	7.8	5.4	8.5	4.2
	Total	10.5	18.3	19.2	28.5	18.0

Jute						
Raw jute (264), jute fabrics (653.4), jute sacks (656.1)	Tariffs	0.0	0.0	—	3.6	3.6
	Transport	41.2	19.7	—	11.9	-29.3
	Total	41.2	19.7	—	15.5	-25.7
Sisal, Henequen						
Raw sisal and henequen (265.4), cordage (655.6)	Tariffs	0.0	—	—	3.6	3.6
	Transport	13.9	—	—	5.6	-8.3
	Total	13.9	—	—	9.2	-4.7
Iron						
Iron ore (281.3), pig iron (671), ingots (672), rolling mill products (673, 676)	Tariffs	0.0	0.7	6.3	3.5	3.5
	Transport	27.7	7.9	4.9	12.0	-15.7
	Total	27.7	8.6	11.2	15.5	-12.2
Copper						
Copper ore (283.1), copper unwrought (682.1), wrought (682.2)	Tariffs	0.1	2.3	—	4.2	4.1
	Transport	3.9	2.0	—	2.8	-1.1
	Total	4.0	4.3	—	7.0	3.0

*Numbers in parentheses show each product's SITC classification.

Source: Alexander J. Yeats, "Do International Transport Costs Increase with Fabrication? Some Empirical Evidence," Oxford Economic Papers 29 (November 1977):462. Reprinted by permission.

factor increases more than 15 percentage points over that for their primary product shipments. Further examination of other data shown in Table 5.7 indicates that the behavior of rubber freight rates should not be considered an isolated example. The average nominal transport costs for the final stage of meat, fish, cocoa, jute, and iron exports are all considerably higher than those registered for the aggregate U.S. import statistics. Overall, these data suggest that the actual behavior of transport costs over processing chains does not stimulate fabrication in developing countries while, in specific instances, shipping costs actually discourage the processing function.

Table 5.8 provides summary data concerning nominal tariff and transport costs for the 21 commodities included in this analysis. Shown here are average ad valorem rates for each processing stage, as well as the percentage point change in freight and tariff charges. The averages for each group have been computed using weights based on developed country imports from developing countries. While these figures have been derived from aggregate U.S. import statistics, with no attempt to hold the mix of exporting countries constant, data in parentheses show similar information for U.S. imports from specific countries.

Overall, the structure of transportation costs appears to intensify somewhat the competitive pressures on U.S. processing concerns. For the all-commodity average, freight rates decline almost five percentage points from the first stage (14 percent) to just over 9 percent for the final stage of fabrication. However, the decline is minor compared with the corresponding increase in tariffs (from 3.5 to 18.2 percent) over this range. The influence of tariffs and transport charges thus produces a series of joint import costs that rise fully 10 percentage points over the four processing stages. A point to be noted is that there are instances where transport costs behave quite differently than indicated by these overall figures. For example, leather, wood, and rubber freight rates rise with processing and reinforce the protective effect of graduated tariffs.

Table 5.8 also presents evidence that the apparent decline of transport rates evidenced in the aggregate trade statistics is largely the result of shifting sources of supply. When similar freight rates are computed for specific developing country shipments, the nominal freight factors fall by only 0.4 percent. Within the levels of accuracy of the data employed in this study, such a figure indicates essentially unchanged nominal transportation costs. However, this overall result is heavily influenced by metals shipments, where transport rates do deescalate considerably. Without the influence of metals in the overall average, nominal transportation rates for shipments from specific countries show increases as one moves to higher levels of fabrication.

TABLE 5.7

Analysis of Ad Valorem Transport and Insurance Costs
on Selected Developing Country Exports,
by Stage of Processing

| Processing Chain | Exporting Countries | Processing Stage | | Percentage Point Change |
		Primary Product	Final Good	
Meat products	All countries	10.1	4.9	-5.2
	Argentina	6.1	5.1	-1.0
	Guatemala	1.5	8.6	7.1
	Nicaragua	6.9	5.0	-1.9
Fish products	All countries	6.8	5.6	-1.2
	India	12.6	12.7	0.1
	Indonesia	9.6	12.7	3.1
	Peru	26.2	22.0	-4.2
	Thailand	8.0	9.5	1.5
Vegetables	All countries	4.3	14.9	10.6
	India	15.9	23.2	7.3
	Haiti	32.0	38.5	6.5
	Philippines	15.9	16.5	0.6
	Turkey	11.3	13.4	2.1
Cocoa	All countries	5.0	8.1	3.1
	Brazil	4.8	20.1	15.3
	Ghana*	5.5	10.2	4.7
	Dominican Republic	4.2	4.2	0.0
Leather	All countries	3.9	9.1	5.2
	Argentina	3.6	6.6	3.0
	Brazil	4.7	6.9	2.2
	Colombia	2.6	8.5	5.9
	Haiti	4.0	5.9	1.9
	India	10.1	21.1	11.0
	Pakistan	4.2	10.3	6.1
Rubber	All countries	9.9	15.6	5.7
	Brazil	8.4	43.2	34.8
	India	10.2	35.0	24.8
	Malaysia	8.9	23.1	14.2
Wood	All countries	2.9	8.6	5.7
	Brazil	13.0	26.9	13.9
	Guatemala	13.2	15.2	2.0

(continued)

TABLE 5.7 (continued)

| Processing Chain | Exporting Countries | Processing stage | | Percentage Point Change |
		Primary Product	Final Good	
Wood	India	16.4	32.0	15.6
(continued)	Indonesia	40.1	29.7	-10.4
Wool	All countries	8.9	9.6	0.7
	Uruguay	5.7	3.9	-1.8
Cotton	All countries	4.3	8.5	4.2
	Brazil	16.8	9.2	-7.6
	India	4.6	8.0	3.4
	Pakistan	20.0	14.9	-5.1
Jute	All countries	41.2	11.9	-29.3
	India	36.0	20.0	-16.0
	Bangladesh	34.2	19.3	-14.9
Iron	All countries	7.9	12.0	4.1
	Brazil	7.5	7.4	-0.1
	India	17.0	46.9	29.9
	Korea	8.3	8.7	0.4
	China, Taiwan	11.8	11.9	0.1
Copper	All countries	3.9	2.8	-1.1
	Peru	4.2	2.3	-1.9
Aluminum	All countries	32.6	6.1	-26.5
	Surinam	50.4	5.1	-45.3
Lead	All countries	6.7	1.4	-5.3
	Peru	14.7	10.9	-3.8

*Ghana's final-stage ad valorem transport rate is for cocoa powder and butter since this country does not export chocolate to the United States.

Source: Alexander J. Yeats, "Do International Transport Costs Increase with Fabrication? Some Empirical Evidence," Oxford Economic Papers 29 (November 1977):465. Reprinted by permission.

TABLE 5.8

Transportation Costs and Nominal Tariffs for U.S. Imports,
by Stage of Processing
(all figures in percent)

Commodity		Stage of Processing				Percentage Point Change[a]
		I	II	III	IV	
Leather	Tariffs	1.1	4.7	7.7	14.0	12.9
	Transport	3.9	4.5	6.2	9.1	5.2 (5.0)
	Total	5.0	9.2	13.9	23.1	18.1 (17.9)
Wood[b]	Tariffs	0.0	0.3	8.1	6.7	6.7
	Transport	2.9	6.7	16.2	8.6	5.7 (5.3)
	Total	2.9	7.0	24.3	15.3	12.4 (12.0)
Textiles[c]	Tariffs	5.8	8.3	14.2	19.1	13.3
	Transport	9.5	11.5	5.9	8.8	-0.7 (-1.5)
	Total	15.3	19.8	20.1	27.9	12.6 (11.8)
Rubber	Tariffs	0.0	4.6	—	—	4.6
	Transport	9.9	15.6	—	—	5.7 (24.6)
	Total	9.9	20.2	—	—	10.3 (29.0)
Food	Tariffs	5.4	6.1	—	—	0.7
	Transport	17.6	9.0	—	—	-8.6 (1.2)
	Total	23.0	15.1	—	—	-7.9 (1.9)
Metals	Tariffs	0.9	4.3	7.8	3.8	2.9
	Transport	24.1	6.3	2.0	11.2	-12.9 (-7.4)
	Total	25.0	10.6	9.8	15.0	-10.0 (-4.4)
All items	Tariffs	3.5	4.4	11.6	18.2	14.7
	Transport	14.0	8.6	8.0	9.2	-4.8 (-0.4)
	Total	17.5	13.0	19.6	27.4	9.9 (14.3)

[a] Figures in parentheses show changes in freight factors for specific countries.

[b] Includes paper and paper products.

[c] Excludes jute and sisal.

Note: Averages shown in this table have been computed using weights based on developed country imports from developing countries.

Source: Alexander J. Yeats, "Do International Transport Costs Increase with Fabrication? Some Empirical Evidence," Oxford Economic Papers 29 (November 1977):468. Reprinted by permission.

Determinants of Freight Rates

The preceding analysis demonstrated that the structure of international transport costs often does not have the beneficial influence on locating processing activities in developing countries that some economists have suggested. However, a key question that was not addressed concerns the reasons why freight charges behave as they do. Specifically, it is of primary importance to determine whether the observed structure of freight charges over processing chains reflects variations in the actual cost of carriage, or an arbitrary rate structure adopted by the liner conferences based on considerations such as "charging what the traffic will bear." If the latter factor is predominant, then the rate-making policies of the liner conferences are in conflict with the industrialization goals of developing countries.

A survey of the existing literature lends support to the proposition of conflict between conference pricing and the objectives of developing countries. For example, an important study by Jan Jansson and Dan Shneerson estimated the long-run marginal cost (LRMC) of shipping various types of commodities and compared these figures with actual liner conference freight rates.[10] The results showed a consistent tendency for LRMCs to lie above actual freight rates for primary and semiprocessed products, while the opposite effect was observed for consumption and investment goods. This led the authors to conclude that

> the principle of charging according to the value of service that is applied by conferences implies that high value commodities subsidize low value commodities. Our results support this hypothesis. Excess freight factors escalate in a manner similar to tariffs. In comparison to a marginal cost-based system of charges, shipping rates tend to encourage trade in raw materials and intermediate goods and to discourage trade in processed commodities (emphasis added).[11]

Several regression studies also shed considerable light on the factors influencing liner freight rates. For example, in one such study for the National Bureau of Economic Research, Robert Lipsey and Merle Weiss conclude that

> there is a commodity structure of transport charges in which the main determinants of these rates are similar over fairly different time periods and trade routes. The main elements we identify as determinants on the cost side are the stowage factor, the distance over which it is

shipped, the size of individual shipments, and the possibility of shipping the product by tanker. <u>The main element in transport charges which we identify with discrimination by shipping companies in rate setting</u> (emphasis added) is the unit value per ton of the commodity.[12]

Given that the authors reject the proposition that a relation exists between the value of a commodity and its true cost-of-carriage, the results of these regression studies, as well as detailed comparisons of conference prices and costs, provide considerable evidence that arbitrary freight rates often discriminate against fabricated goods.

Finally, it must be noted that another body of studies also shows that liner conference freight rates typically discriminate against processed commodities. Specifically, individual studies of liner conference pricing practices have consistently shown that "charging what the traffic will bear" is normally a key factor influencing the structure of freight rates. As summarized by B. M. Deakin: "Shipping conferences do not set prices with reference to social, or even private cost, at least not predominantly. Rather they fix their prices with regard to the strengths or weakness of demand for the carriage of particular types of goods, using the principle generally referred to 'charging what the traffic will bear'." As such, the difference between the actual cost-of-carriage and the tariff applied by the conference is greater for high valued (processed) items than for primary unprocessed goods. This results in a lower proportion of processed good exports than would occur under a pricing system based on true cost conditions.

Transport Cost Estimation Equations

The findings of the various studies dealing with international transport costs have a direct bearing on rational planning of export ventures. Since ad valorem freight rates often escalate, and assume considerably higher levels than tariffs, the magnitude and structure of shipping costs may mean the difference between success or failure of a new export venture. However, rational planning becomes difficult when reliable information on transport costs is not available in advance of the product's introduction. In this respect, recent studies concerning transport cost estimation equations may provide valuable insights concerning the probable dimensions of transport costs for such exports.

An illustrative example is the study by Lipsey and Weiss.[14] The authors start with the premise that U.S. import freight rates

(FR) expressed in dollars per ton can largely be explained by the following equation, where all variables are in logarithmic form,

$$FR = 3.53 + 0.52 \, UV + 0.30 \, DI + 0.35 \, ST$$
$$\qquad\quad (57.35) \qquad (13.51) \qquad (18.18)$$

$$\qquad + \; 0.30 \, SW - 0.51 \, TA$$
$$\qquad\quad (6.22) \qquad (12.25)$$

where UV is the unit value ($ per ton), DI is the distance in nautical miles, ST is the stowage factor (cubic feet per ton), SW is a dummy variable for a shipment of less than one ton, and TA is a dummy for products that can be imported by both liners and tankers, that is, grains and other similar products. The t values (in parentheses) and a coefficient of determination (R^2) of over 80 percent testify to the accurate guide that such an equation can provide to freight rates for individual products.

Further information about the utility of such equations for predicting transport costs is presented in Table 5.9. Shown here are estimated freight rates using equation 5.1 along with reported freight charges. In general, the actual and projected rates are in rather close agreement, but where differences exist, there are logical explanations. For example, no variable is included in equation 5.1 to account for product fragility; this omission probably accounts for the underestimates in freight rates for glassware and pottery and may also be a factor for toys, games, and alcoholic beverages.*

Variations in the regression model can be tested, with the final results used for estimating transport costs for the new export ventures being contemplated. Since the explanatory variables all relate to product and other characteristics known in advance (that is, unit values, stowage factors, distance, and so on) these can be utilized to make the required projections. However, it should be noted that there are other potential uses of such equations that have received

---

*Due to the upward trend in freight rates, an effort must be made to employ the most recent data available for estimating equation 5.1. If, say, 1975 data were used, the projected freight rates would contain a serious downward bias due to the general increase in transport costs since that period. An effort should also be made to estimate transport cost equations for each of the individual export markets since Lipsey and Weiss present somewhat different results for Germany as opposed to the United States.

TABLE 5.9

Actual and Estimated Transport Charges:
Averages by Major Commodity Groups
(dollars per metric ton)

| SITC | Description | Average Freight Change | |
		Reported	Estimated
011	Fresh and frozen meat	87	66
013	Prepared meat	50	64
031	Fresh and frozen fish	69	65
051	Fresh fruits and nuts	24	27
061	Sugar and honey	8	10
071	Coffee	40	52
081	Animal feeds	25	20
112	Alcoholic beverages	64	50
231	Crude rubber	51	44
262	Wool	90	103
281	Iron ore	2	2
283	Nonferrous ores	5	4
331	Petroleum, crude	2	3
332	Refined petroleum	2	2
422	Fixed vegetable oils	15	29
512	Organic chemicals	31	30
631	Plywood and veneers	39	34
653	Textile fabrics	87	105
664	Glass	33	29
665	Glassware	173	87
666	Pottery	92	60
674	Iron and steel plates	19	14
732	Motor vehicles	130	109
841	Clothing	254	260
851	Footwear	196	171
861	Scientific instruments	319	311
894	Sporting goods	270	189
899	Manufactured articles	201	169

Source: Robert Lipsey and Merle Weiss, "The Structure of Ocean Transport Charges," Explorations in Economic Research 1 (Summer 1974):167. Reprinted by permission.

attention. Specifically, if projected rates are consistently below actual transport costs for a group of products or countries, this could identify areas for further research on the potential factors (such as discrimination) causing such variations. Estimation of such equations at different time intervals could also provide useful insights into the influence of the various factors leading to freight cost changes.

NOTES

1. UNCTAD, The Processing Before Export of Primary Commodities: Areas for Further International Co-operation (TD/229/supp. 2) (Manila: United Nations, 1979).

2. R. Bosson and B. Varon, The Minerals Industry in Developing Countries (London: Oxford University Press, 1977).

3. Alberto Valdes, Trade Liberalization in Agricultural Commodities and the Potential Foreign Exchange Benefits to Developing Countries (Washington, D.C.: International Food Policy Research Institute, 1979); and Alexander J. Yeats, "Effective Protection for Processed Agricultural Commodities," Journal of Economics and Business 29 (Fall 1977):31-39.

4. See UNCTAD, The Kennedy Round Estimated Effects on Tariff Barriers (New York: United Nations, 1970).

5. Odd Gulbrandsen and Assar Lindbeck, The Economics of the Agricultural Sector (Stockholm: Almqvist and Wicksell, 1973).

6. World Bank, World Development Report (Washington, D.C.: World Bank, 1978).

7. UNCTAD, Marketing and Distribution System for Cocoa (TD/B/C.1/164) (Geneva: United Nations, 1975).

8. For more detailed discussions of this problem, see UNCTAD, Towards the Technological Transformation of the Developing Countries (TD/238) (Manila: UNCTAD, 1979).

9. UNCTAD, The Processing Before Export of Primary Commodities.

10. Jan Jansson and Dan Shneerson, "The Effective Protection Implicit in Liner Rate Shipping," Review of Economics and Statistics 60 (November 1978):569-73.

11. Ibid., p.

12. Robert E. Lipsey and Merle Y. Weiss, "The Structure of Ocean Transport Charges," Explorations in Economic Research 1 (Summer 1974):178. Similar results showing product value to be a major determinant of freight rates were achieved by Carmellah Moneta, "The Estimation of Transport Costs in International Trade," Journal of Political Economy 67 (February 1959):41-58; and Ingrid Bryan, "Ocean Liner Freight Rates," Journal of Transport Economics and Policy 8 (May 1974):161-73.

13. B. M. Deakin, "Shipping Conferences, Some Economic Aspects of International Regulation," Maritime Studies and Management 2 (May 1974):11. Similar conclusions concerning pricing practices have been reached in a number of other studies dealing with the conferences.

6

POLICY PERSPECTIVES ON
TRANSPORT

A central theme running through the preceding chapters is
that far more attention must be devoted to transport costs in trade
and development planning than has generally been assumed. It was
shown that developing countries' ad valorem freight rates consistently
exceed corresponding tariffs, often by considerable margins, and
that ad valorem transport costs often escalate with processing. Given
the important influence freight rates have on the level and structure
of developing country exports, a key question centers on the degree
to which they are subject to some degree of control.

Along with mounting evidence on the true importance of transport costs as trade barriers, there has been an increased realization
that transport problems may be approached by various policy measures.
The proposals that have been advanced are generally aimed at stimulating increased competition in shipping markets, or improving the
efficiency and operation of existing transport services. Special attention has been given to the establishment of national fleets, improving
existing transport services as well as the adoption of new technologies, improving the bargaining position of shippers relative to shipowners, or the establishment of a "code of conduct" for liner conferences. The following sections of this chapter consider the rationale
behind and prospects for success of policy prescriptions in these areas.

DEVELOPMENT OF NATIONAL FLEETS

One of UNCTAD's policy recommendations concerning developing country transport problems centered on the establishment of national shipping fleets. This was partly the result of several studies
in the early 1960s that showed transport and insurance costs were a
significant drain on developing country foreign exchange reserves
(see Table 1.2). These studies led to the realization that if shipping
services were provided by national fleets, some payments, such as

seamen's wages, could be made in local currencies, thus involving substantial foreign exchange savings.

Aside from the foreign exchange effects, other reasons have been advanced for developing countries to establish national fleets. These include:

Prevention of service disruptions during hostilities: A country dependent on foreign shipping faces the risk that its trade may be disrupted during hostilities. Even during hostilities in which a country does not take part, as was the case of Brazil in World War II, it may experience severe disruptions in trade due to changes in the supply of shipping capacity. In such cases, a national fleet could service key imports and exports.

Reduction of economic dependence: A country having no national fleet must rely on foreign shipowners for its foreign trade. Commercial profitability normally is the primary consideration of individual shipowners and, should a given country's trade not provide sufficient profits, the possibility exists that transport services might be withdrawn, or provided in old or unsuitable vessels, or only at a very high price. By having its own merchant fleet, a country could minimize such risks.

Influencing conference decisions: With its own merchant fleet, a country can claim the right to participate in liner conferences affecting its trade, thus acquiring a position to influence conference decisions concerning freight rates and matters pertaining to transport policy.

Economic integration: In countries with a long coastline or with difficult internal communications, such as the Philippines, national shipping may be the only effective link between major metropolitan or commercial centers.

Export promotion: Some developing countries have used national flagships, often government-owned, to promote trade in new products or with new partners. Their experience shows that national lines take a more sympathetic view toward promotional freight rates, which can be of key importance in new export ventures.

Diversification of employment: Some countries have taken an integrated approach toward establishment of national fleets through the promotion of shipbuilding activities. Actively encouraging domestic construction of national fleets may also have important linkage effects on employment and secondary production.

National Fleets and Collective Self-Reliance

In recent years some developing country spokesmen have increasingly advocated that these nations pursue industrialization policies based on the concept of collective self-reliance. This strategy centers on the proposition that by increasing commercial, financial, political, and other cooperative contacts, developing countries could weaken the influence that developed countries exercise on their economic policies and have considerably more freedom to pursue national development objectives.[1]

One key barrier to expanded intratrade and collective self-reliance is that established liner routes may not allow many developing countries to engage in direct trade contacts. This is unfortunate since the export structures of many newly industrialized countries of Asia and South America suggest that there are numerous potential trade opportunities between these nations. However, few possibilities for direct trade contacts exist since established liner routes generally necessitate costly transshipment through a commercial center. Such shipment may offset the comparative cost advantage that developing countries have in the production of their exports.[*]

The problem of transport costs for developing country intratrade may also be severe on an intraregional basis. As with interregional trade, this is because existing institutions have evolved to service a North-South flow of goods. Even among neighboring developing countries, the established links for communication and trade may normally be from the interior of the country to a port, and then directly outward to a metropolitan center.

A recent investigation by Wilfred Prewo provides information on the importance of transport problems as a barrier to intratrade.[2] Using this information, Table 6.1 shows ad valorem freight rates for Latin American intratrade. Before examining these data, however, several points should be noted. First, the freight factors are for aggregate trade flows and have been derived using actual trade weights. This invariably leads to a downward bias in such estimates since trade in items bearing high transport charges is depressed because of the influence of these costs. As such, the high-transport-cost products enter the overall average with relatively low weights.

---

[*]There is no single satisfactory information source for tracing the full pattern of established liner routes. This problem deserves far more attention than it has received given the importance being attached to the concept of collective self-reliance. A publication by Croners provides the most comprehensive tabulation of conferences serving given developing countries and given industrial countries, although it does not provide any data on way-port stops along the route.[3] See U. S. Croners, Reference Book for Shippers (New York: Croner Publishers, various issues).

TABLE 6.1

Average Ad Valorem Transport Costs for Eight Latin American Countries' Aggregate Trade with Other Developing Nations

Importing Country	Exporting Country							
	Argentina	Brazil	Colombia	Chile	Mexico	Peru	Uruguay	Venezuela
Argentina	—	19.6	93.9	12.9	10.3	7.1	7.1	55.0
Brazil	19.1	—	—	13.4	27.1	—	26.8	216.9
Colombia	31.6	8.8	—	9.3	14.4	11.7	4.7	38.4
Costa Rica	—	—	142.5	9.9	20.1	—	—	191.8
Chile	8.4	17.0	7.2	—	16.3	8.6	15.7	216.4
Ecuador	15.4	52.2	9.8	14.6	13.2	—	—	45.0
Mexico	8.8	47.4	25.0	37.5	—	21.7	—	—
Peru	11.9	53.7	10.9	24.5	9.1	—	—	—
Uruguay	38.5	43.1	—	13.2	10.5	—	—	—
Venezuela	22.0	21.0	12.9	3.5	6.5	95.0	—	—
El Salvador	—	—	62.9	5.9	24.7	—	—	—
Guatemala	21.9	84.1	5.6	13.5	12.0	—	—	176.7
Honduras	—	54.0	5.7	—	8.0	—	—	—
Nicaragua	—	83.5	15.0	—	26.5	—	45.0	—
Panama	14.0	—	5.8	15.9	39.4	11.5	8.2	92.8
Dominican Republic	19.6	—	22.9	—	—	—	—	—
Trinidad and Tobago	16.7	40.0	—	27.3	—	—	—	23.0

Source: Adapted from Wilfred Prewo, "The Structure of Transport Costs on Latin American Exports," Welt-wirtschaftliches Archiv 114, no. 2:324. Reprinted by permission.

A second point is that the figures refer to freight costs for intraregional trade. Since many of these countries' ports may be serviced by interlinking routes, costly transshipment may not be involved. Also, the distances involved may be less than in interregional trade. Transshipment and longer hauls could lead to higher transport rates than shown in the table.

In spite of these qualifications, some ad valorem freight costs for intratrade are very high. Colombian exports to Argentina have freight factors of over 90 percent, while rates of 142 percent are experienced on the former's shipments to Costa Rica. Venezuela's trade with other developing countries often incurs transport factors of 100 to 200 percent or more, while rates of 40 to 100 percent occur throughout the matrix. Since evidence shows that direct shipments from developed countries such as the United States often face markedly lower transport costs, differential freight rates constitute an important barrier to intratrade.*

While adverse freight rate differentials, by themselves, may constitute an important obstacle to intratrade, their interaction with tariffs has a further detrimental effect. For example, Figure 6.1

---

*For example, Sidney Dell notes that

the high cost of transport between Latin American ports has seriously impeded the development of area trade: in many cases it is cheaper to ship goods from Europe or North America than between points within the region. For example, the freight rate for lumber shipped from Mexico to Venezuela was $24 per ton as compared to $11 per ton from Finland to Venezuela, even though the distance is three times greater. From Buenos Aires to Tampico, Mexico the ocean freight rate for chemicals was $54 per ton for direct shipment; but if the goods were trans-shipped in New Orleans the rate was only $46, while trans-shipment in Southampton, England, brought down the rate further to $40, despite the tremendous increases in distances involved. Nor is it simply a question of high costs. Goods shipped from Porto Alegre in Brazil to Montevideo actually reach their destination more quickly if sent via Hamburg, West Germany. In fact Uruguayan wool is shipped to the United States by way of Hamburg even when there are ships available going directly to New York.[4]

FIGURE 6.1

Diagrammatic Analysis of the Relation between
Freight and Tariff Differentials under a
Cost-Insurance-Freight Valuation Base

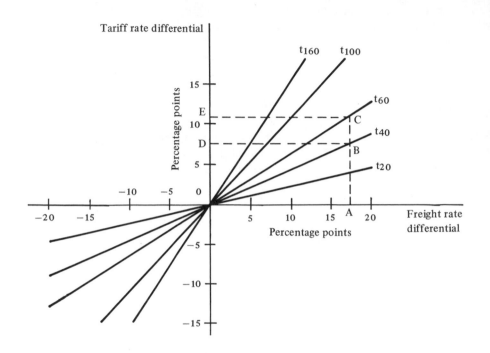

Source: Constructed by the author.

illustrates this interaction between freight rates and the c.i.f. tariff valuation system. The horizontal axis measures various possible freight rate differentials facing developing countries on intratrade, while the vertical axis shows associated tariff differentials. As such, observations in the upper-right quadrant match adverse developing country freight margins with adverse tariff differentials. The lines such as t_{20} trace out the relation between tariff and freight rate differentials at various tariff levels.* For example, a freight rate differential of 18 percent (OA) in connection with a 60 percent tariff rate would produce an adverse tariff margin of over 10 percentage points (OE). Figure 6.1 also shows that the c.i.f. system <u>may</u> produce a tariff differential in favor of developing countries. While available evidence suggests this is an exception, some trade involving neighboring countries may have lower transport costs than involved in trade with nations in different geographic regions. Situations in which freight and tariff margins work in favor of developing country intratrade are shown in the lower left-hand quadrant of the figure.

While one potential solution to the tariff discrimination problem might suggest removal of the transport cost component from the valuation base, that is, apply customs duties on an f.o.b. basis, there are situations where this may have some localized unfavorable effects. Specifically, transport costs between some neighboring countries may be lower than on shipments between the developing countries and industrial nations. Even though these situations are not likely to occur with a high frequency, adoption of a strict f.o.b. valuation base could alter the tariff system in favor of developed countries in these instances.

As an alternative, a dual import valuation system could be employed that would <u>always</u> generate trade preferences in favor of developing countries as a group. Specifically, if imports from developing countries were valued using an f.o.b. tariff base (such as that employed in the United States), while imports from developed countries were taxed under a c.i.f. procedure (used by the EEC and Japan), this two-tier system will always favor developing country intratrade as a whole.† Aside from the preference-generating

---

*The tariff differential for developing country i over developed country j in the kth developing country market (T_{ik}) can be derived from

$$T_{ik} = t(f_{ik} - f_{dk})\qquad\qquad 6.1$$

where t is the tariff rate applied by developing country k, f_{ik} is the ad valorem freight rate for shipments from i to k, while f_{dk} is the ad valorem freight rate for exports from the developed country.

†Equation (6.1) shows why this must be the case. Essentially, the two-tier system results in setting the term f_{ik} equal to zero. Given nonzero transport costs for exports from developed to developing countries, this is sufficient to cause T_{ik} to be negative, that is, always to generate preferences in favor of the developing countries.

ability of such a proposal, another attraction is that it removes the adverse tariff effects associated with the present c.i.f. system. As such, the two-tier system is more effective than other plans that might be considered (such as a linear cut to establish preferential margins) since these alternative proposals fail to fully offset the detrimental effects of the interaction of c.i.f. tariffs and freight costs.

While adjustments in the valuation base would offset some of the problems developing countries face on intratrade, it cannot fully counter the disadvantages associated with existing institutional factors in shipping. To attack these basic problems the developing countries will have to acquire more influence in matters relating to the transport of their international trade.

Since a major contribution could come from the expansion of national fleets, policies should be pursued to increase the role of developing countries in shipping. In this respect, the phasing out of open registry fleets could be significant since there is reason to believe that many of the vessels registered in this category would transfer to developing countries. The anticompetitive practices of the liner conferences are also a major constraint as developing countries often are unable to achieve membership in these closed cartels. It is one of the major objectives of the Liner Conference Code of Conduct to increase developing country participation in the conferences that service their national trade.

Aside from institutional factors, another barrier that is assuming steadily increasing importance relates to financial requirements for the purchase of new vessels. As shown in Table 6.2, new vessel prices have increased dramatically over the last decade with the construction cost for an 11,000- to 13,000-dwt liner-type vessel rising by 280 percent (to $11.4 million in 1979). While the price rise has been less dramatic, the table shows that bulk carrier and tanker costs often range between $20 and $60 million, and reach $125 million for a modern liquefied natural gas carrier. Obviously, if the developing countries are to expand shipping operations they will require assistance from international lending institutions such as the World Bank, given the imposing magnitude of the capital costs involved.*

---

*Apart from export credits, bilateral aid agencies, international institutions, and commercial banks, UNCTAD suggests the possibility of financing ship purchases by transporting cargoes to the country supplying the vessels. As an example, a Chilean company recently purchased an ore-oil carrier from Japan for a triangular operation involving Chile-Japan (ore), Japan-Gulf (ballast), and Gulf-Chile (oil), on the basis that the purchase price will be canceled by nonpayment of freight on the Chile-Japan run over a ten-year period.

TABLE 6.2

Representative New Building Prices for Various Types of Vessels in 1970, 1973, 1976, and 1979
(millions of dollars)

Type of Vessel	1970	1973	1976	1979	Percentage change, 1970–79
30,000-dwt bulk carrier	8.7	12.0	11.0	15.5	78.1
30,000-dwt tanker	10.0	17.5	15.0	23.0	130.0
70,000-dwt bulk carrier	11.9	20.5	16.0	26.0	118.5
87,000-dwt tanker	17.0	25.0	16.0	30.0	76.5
96,000-dwt OBO[a]	23.0	29.0	23.0	35.0	52.1
120,000-dwt bulk carrier	17.2	31.0	24.0	33.0	91.9
210,000-dwt tanker	31.0	47.0	34.0	45.0	45.2
400,000-dwt tanker	—	78.0	56.0	60.0	—
125,000-m^3 LNG carrier	—	105.0	105.0	125.0	—
75,000-m^3 LPG carrier	—	45.0	42.0	60.0	—
5,000-dwt ro/ro	5.3	9.8	10.0	14.0	164.2
11,000- to 13,000-dwt liner type vessel	3.0	5.0	9.2	11.4	280.0

[a] A vessel that has the capability of transporting ore, bulk cargoes, or oil.

[b] Construction prices originally stated in terms of pounds sterling and converted to dollars at the ratio of $2.2 equals £1.

Source: UNCTAD, Review of Maritime Transport, various issues.

COMPETITION AND THE QUALITY OF
SHIPPING SERVICES

Economic theory and empirical research show that the degree
of competition in a market is directly related to the number and size
distribution of operating units. The smaller the number of operating
units, and the more unequal their size distribution, the lower is the
probability that there will be aggressive competition. The importance
of stimulating or maintaining competition is that a competitive system generally yields lower prices and profits than one in which aggressive competition is absent.

Numerous studies have attempted to measure the influence
of market competition or structure on performance. With some
measure of profits as an indicator of performance, and the concentration ratio as a proxy for the size distribution of firms, a statistically significant positive relationship has been found in these studies
between industry profits and the level of concentration.[5] The message that emerges from these studies is that consumers clearly benefit from increased competition in the markets they rely on, while
competition also leads to the adoption of more efficient production
procedures. The consistency of these findings is particularly impressive in view of the fact that different testing techniques, different
profit performance measures, different measures of concentration,
different samples, and various levels of aggregation have been used.
It should also be noted that the empirical findings concerning the
beneficial effects of competition have held for all types of industrial,
commercial, service, or financial markets.

Imperfections in International Markets

While the primary focus of the market structure performance
relation has been on the domestic markets of industrial nations, recent extensions of this work also show that the conclusions apply to
international markets that are subject to a high degree of monopoly
control. Specifically, it has been found that if foreign markets of
developing countries are dominated by one or a few sellers or buyers,
these nations receive less favorable terms for their imports or exports than would be the case if aggressive competition prevailed.[6]

A variety of factors relating to finance, transportation, cul-
ture, and the historic pattern of development often tie developing
countries to one or a few metropolitan states. As noted, liner conferences have often established routes between given developing
nations and one, or a relatively few, industrial countries so the
potential for broadened trade contacts is limited by existing transport

services. Language, financial ties, as well as established marketing and distribution systems are frequently such that developing countries have little external flexibility in trade relations. Finally, the export structures of many developing countries, centering on the production of primary goods and raw materials, have developed historically to serve the needs of a metropolitan state. This specialized pattern of commerce works to further limit the trading possibilities. Industrial nations, in contrast, normally have considerably broader contacts and more diversified trade structures; so their dependence on any one developing country is limited.

In short, the normal situation is one in which a developing country disposes of its exports in a market characterized by varying degrees of monopoly power, while imports of manufactures and capital equipment are subject to control by one or a few metropolitan states. In this environment the power to influence commercial relations clearly lies with the developed nations. The marketing and distribution systems for many developing country products are also controlled by elements based in industrial nations. This adds to the potential for abuse of monopoly power that would work against the developing countries. Much of the debate concerning the new international order centers on ways to redress the vast imbalances in economic power between developed and developing countries. Clearly, ways in which these differences can be reduced must be given highest priority.

There is little doubt that the institutional factors in shipping have an important retardation effect on much potentially beneficial competition that could occur in developing countries' import and export trade. Aside from North-South trade routes, the practices of the conferences (such as loyalty contracts, deferred rebates, and so on) do much to foreclose competition in freight markets. Because of the peculiar institutional arrangements in liner shipping, it is not possible for those utilizing these services to trust that competition will moderate prices charged for shipping services to a reasonable margin above cost levels. Nor is it possible to rely upon pressure from competitors and consumers to force shipowners to increase efficiency so that cost levels are reduced.

Given existing institutional constraints, questions arise as to what developing countries can do to impart a greater degree of competition in their freight markets. The UNCTAD Secretariat has made a number of general policy proposals concerning this matter. First, to strengthen the country's bargaining power it is suggested that shippers be organized, either by establishing a shippers' council or by other appropriate means, and that consultation procedures be established to ensure that shippers' interests be considered. Second, for the purpose of assessing the efficiency of existing transport services, the extent to which shipping is affecting the country's trade, and the possibility of obtaining more satisfactory services, a shipping investigative unit should be established. Third, in order to ensure that the country is not making unnecessary use of relatively expensive liner services for cargoes that could move by charter or contract methods, traditional liner consignments should be aggregated if possible. Also, to deal with foreign exchange aspects of transport problems, as well as to inject a new competitive element into the market, consideration should be given to the establishment of national fleets.

The Role of Shippers' Councils

Although a prime function of a shippers' council is to improve the bargaining position of exporters, it can also have an important operational role in enabling shippers to form a collective approach, and in acting as their spokesman. Beneficial changes in shipping, covering both institutional changes and daily operational matters, can be blocked through the lack of any means of obtaining the collective participation of shippers, and this problem can be alleviated by a shippers' council. However, experience shows that shippers' councils may also make beneficial changes by establishing an investigative unit to analyze different aspects of shipping services afforded exporters.[7]

With regard to the work of such a unit, UNCTAD suggests that its main concern will be with cargoes currently transported by liners. This is justified by the view that problems in the nonliner sector are relatively straightforward, while those that arise within the liner sector are widespread and relatively complex. For example, shippers who utilize charter or contract methods can usually be relied upon to arrange for the most economical services available unless they are prevented by inadequate port or marshalling arrangements. If this were the case, they could bring their complaints to the shippers' council investigation unit. The required analysis would be relatively straightforward with the basic question being whether the benefits resulting from an improvement in facilities, that is, a reduction in rate levels and an improvement in the country's competitive position in overseas markets, outweigh the cost of the improvements.

In the liner sector, data relating to common shipping problems are normally lacking and must be compiled, especially in three basic areas: cargo flows, vessels used and their movements, and the requirements of merchants. While the range of problems is likely to vary from country to country, experience shows that the following subjects are likely to be major concerns for the investigative unit:

rationalization of sailings, possible use of containers or new systems, efficiency of individual carriers, preparation of cargo by shippers, aggregation of consignments, the use of nonconference liner services, and the feasible development of national fleets.

TECHNICAL FACTORS IN SHIPPING

Any analysis of the technological changes in shipping over the last few decades must conclude that these advances have the capacity to alter the level and structure of developing country freight rates. While there have been improvements in vessel design, introduction of new and more efficient types of carriers, or refinements in related port facilities, the major innovations that have occurred relate to the fuller and more efficient utilization of existing cargo-carrying capacity. These developments are directed primarily at the reduction of idle port time, which constitutes a major element in total transport costs.

The importance of fixed costs associated with berth time can be appreciated by noting that, on average, a general cargo liner spends about 60 percent of its working life in harbor. However, there may be some variation in this figure due to differences in technical equipment and the efficiency of the ports concerned. Also, Figure 6.2 shows that the length of the liner run has an influence on fixed costs and berth time. If the one-way liner route is 10,000 miles, the chart shows that approximately 50 percent of a ship's time is spent in port, but for shorter routes of about 2,000 miles, the berth time rises to over 80 percent.*

Several studies show the effect of reducing idle berth time on freight rates. For example, R. Goss has estimated that by reducing the time spent in harbor from 60 to 20 percent of operating time it would be possible to lower freight rates by 18 to 35 percent.[8] Similar conclusions were reached by P. Harff, who estimated that by shortening the duration of a voyage (berth plus operating time) by

---

*These calculations are based on the assumption of an average speed of 22 knots, a ship capacity of 9,000 net registered tonnage, and a transshipment capacity for general cargo of 1,000 long tons per day. It should also be noted that due largely to complementary loading and unloading facilities, tramps average about 40 percent of their working life in port while the figure for tankers is estimated at between 15 and 20 percent.

FIGURE 6.2

The Relation between Turnround Time to Transport
Distance for General Cargo Freighters

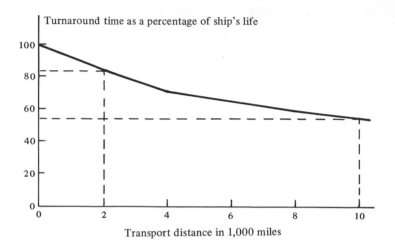

Source: McKinsey & Co., Containerization—The Key to Low
Cost Transport (London: McKinsey, 1967), p. 14.

one-third, ocean transport costs could normally be reduced by about
25 percent.[9] Given the general acceptance of these conclusions,
considerable attention has been directed at the application of technological advances in shipping for reducing idle berth time.

The Containerization Approach

    While there are variations of the unitized approach, the basic
idea behind each is that as much packing as possible be done independent of the ship's presence so that costly berth time is reduced.
The objective is to prepackage manufactured goods in specially built
steel containers so that a homogenous cargo is produced that, given
appropriate handling equipment, can be loaded in a fraction of the
time required for a regular liner vessel. Of the various types of
container systems, lift-on/lift-off cellular container ships make up
the largest group. These vessels are specially constructed or
adapted for the carriage of containers with fixed vertical cellular

guide installations and other container handling features.* Variations in vessel design exist in that "full" container ships devote all, or almost all, of their capacity to containers, while "part" container ships have only a portion of their capacity so utilized.

Aside from cellular container ships, there are other types of unit load carriers. Multipurpose vessels have been constructed to carry a range of unitized cargoes such as containers, vehicles, palletized, break-bulk, or bulk cargoes. The use of these multipurpose vessels provides shipowners with flexibility in meeting varying operating needs over different trade routes. Another variety of unitized transport vessels are barge carriers such as LASH ships (meaning lighters aboard ship), which have the capacity to lift smaller-water carriers (lighters) directly on or off the mother ship. As is the case with cellular containerships, packaging of lighters is done independently of the primary carrier.

Another type of containerized shipping is roll-on/roll-off vessels that accommodate wheeled carriers such as cars, trains, trucks, or roll-on container units. While these vessels were originally designed for short-haul operations, their use has been extended to the Europe-North America, Australia-North America, Australia-Japan, and Australia-Europe routes.

In commenting on the different types of unitized transport modes, mention must also be made of the pallet-based system. This transport mode is based on the horizontal movement of pallets aboard ship by the use of forklift trucks, replacing the traditional vertical movement by ship- or shore-based cranes. This alternative form of cargo unitization, which normally does not have the heavy capital requirements of other container ships, makes them attractive to developing countries.

Given these different forms of unitization, a key question centers on the potential magnitude of the savings that may result from their adoption, and their impact on developing countries. Concerning this latter point, there is still no general agreement on whether they

---

*These technological advances have been accompanied by dramatic increases in the cost of shipping tonnage. While one cubic foot of carrying capacity cost $7 to $8 in the early 1960s, it now costs between $25 and $30. Profitability is now also very sensitive to capacity utilization. For example, at 25 percent capacity utilization the average cost per container in 1974 was $2,228. However, if the load factor were 50 percent the average cost would be $1,240, while that for a fully loaded vessel was $747.

will have a beneficial or detrimental effect on developing country transport objectives. On the one hand, it is acknowledged that unitization may have the capacity to reduce freight rates by 25 percent or more on some runs. However, the required investments in unitized transport modes, along with complementary loading and unloading facilities, may be justified only on routes with relatively large volumes of goods to be transported. These requirements may lead to the adoption of the unitized transport systems primarily for developed countries that have relatively large intratrade. As a result the unitized approach may primarily lower transport costs on developed country intratrade and in the largest developing country ports. This could undercut the position of smaller developing country exporters that do not have access to these new systems.*

Rationalization of Shipping Services

Aside from the introduction of new technologies such as unitized shipping, transport cost savings may result from a more logical planning of the frequency and types of shipping services employed. Cost-saving changes may be possible for the pattern of existing liner routes, the consignment of cargoes, or the types and sizes of vessels utilized. However, the basic idea behind such modifications is to make more efficient use of existing or available shipping services.

An area that often has considerable potential for rationalization is the pattern of actual liner routes. The reason why certain countries are grouped into "trades" for the purposes of liner shipping may be historical and have little relation to efficiency considerations. Individual carriers may have begun to serve a range of ports because their clients had cargoes for that range, yet the overall cargo

---

*Stephen Neff sees these developments leading to a two-tier shipping system in which a "big league of long-distance, capital-intensive, high volume vessels connects a network of superports," while a "little league" of shippers evolves to handle transverse trade between the superports and the countries of ultimate destination of the cargo. For various reasons he sees developing country fleets operating largely in these latter routes.[10] Admittedly, developing countries might achieve transport volumes sufficient to justify investment in unitized shipping systems through the promotion of regional ports. However, no practical attempt has yet been made to establish such ports.

movements may be such that there is no logical basis for combining the entire range of ports into a single trade. If a conference trade covers, say, eight to ten countries, it may be possible that the overall cargo movement could be effected more economically if the route were, say, split into two or more separate trades. No generalizations can be offered due to individual country differences, but the route patterns of some developing countries' trade may be far less than optimal and warrant corrective action.

Aside from the question of routes, possibilities for savings through modification of existing services may exist. For example, bulking or consolidation of cargoes may offer possibilities for transport cost savings. If smaller consignments can be aggregated, less frequent liner calls may be required while the larger bulked cargoes may make more efficient use of existing liner capacity. Aggregation of cargoes may also enhance the bargaining position of shippers since, by jointly negotiating terms for the larger shipment, they may be able to qualify for quantity discounts or somewhat offset the monopoly power of the conferences. Other advantages associated with economies of scale in shipping may also be achieved by bulking and shipment of larger consignments. Transport economists are generally agreed that such economies exist for a wide variety of goods like sugar, timber, rubber, oilseeds, ores, and other products traditionally exported by developing countries.

As an illustration of the cost reductions associated with larger cargoes, Table 6.3 provides an illustration of the potential orders of savings that can be realized through the shift to bigger vessels for the carriage of manganese ore. As shown, the employment of a 25,000-dwt vessel instead of a general cargo vessel of 12,000-15,000 dwg might reduce ocean transport costs by approximately 30 percent. By further increasing the ship size to about 35,000 tons, the potential freight saving rises to 40 percent as compared with the general cargo vessel.* Even a change from 25,000 to 35,000 dwt reduces costs by about 15 percent. When unit costs are expressed on a ton per mile basis it is apparent that transport costs decrease with increased

---

*Various constraints may operate to prevent effective utilization of larger carriers. Aside from limits imposed by local production capacity or in the consumer markets, some ports may not be able to accommodate the larger carriers. However, the message that emerges from the studies of transport scale economies is that, where feasible, developing countries should investigate the possible use of larger carriers.

TABLE 6.3

Estimated Unit Transportation Costs of Manganese Ore Per Ton–Mile and Per Cargo–Ton by Vessel Size and by Trade Route (dollars)

Trade Route	Distance in Nautical Miles	Ship Size (in dwt)				
		12,000	15,000	25,000	35,000	60,000
Estimated cost per cargo–ton						
Brazil–U.S. Atlantic Coast	3,000	8.25	7.75	5.45	4.60	3.70
West Africa–Continent	4,900	13.30	12.60	8.95	7.60	6.25
East Coast of India–Japan	5,000	13.20	12.45	8.85	7.30	6.15
Australia–Continent	12,800	31.95	30.20	21.45	18.15	14.90
Estimated cost per ton–mile						
Brazil–U.S. Atlantic Coast	3,000	0.279	0.263	0.185	0.156	0.125
West Africa–Continent	4,900	0.274	0.259	0.184	0.157	0.129
East Coast of India–Japan	5,000	0.267	0.251	0.179	0.147	0.124
Australia–Continent	12,800	0.245	0.229	0.164	0.139	0.114

Source: UNCTAD, Freight Rates: The Maritime Transportation of Manganese Ore (Geneva: UNCTAD, July 1976), p. 23.

FIGURE 6.3

Iron Ore and Oil Transport Costs as Functions of Vessel Size
(cost per ton on a 20,000-dwt vessel = 100)
Cost relationships of the mid-1960s

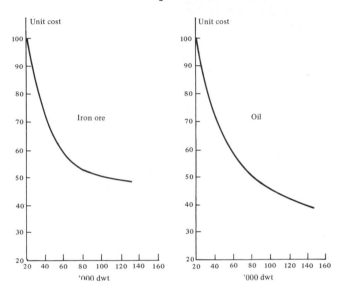

Note: On 5,000-mile routes, empty return voyage, 1965 data.
Although the basic assumptions regarding amortization, interest
rates, and so on, are not identical for oil and ore transport, they are
roughly comparable.
Source: UNCTAD, Protection of Shipper Interests (TD/B/C.4/
127) (Geneva: UNCTAD, 1975), p. 42.

shipping distance, as well as with vessel size. Ton-mile costs are
between 0.1 and 0.3 cents, varying with voyage length and vessel size.
For bulk carriers of about 25,000 dwt, employed in the Brazilian and
West African manganese ore trades, the figure is under 0.2 cents per
ton-mile, while the ton-mile costs would decline further for the larger
sizes or longer trades, the savings being greatest in the longer trades.[*]

---

[*]Scale economies achieved by varying vessel size are based
on the relationship of carrying capacity to building and capital costs,
personnel costs, insurance, bunkers, and stores. For most of these
elements the unit costs of larger vessels are significantly lower.
For example, the number of men required to run a tanker does not
increase proportionately with the size of the vessel.

This explains the use of larger vessels in the trades from Brazil and West Africa, from Australia to the United States, and from South Africa to certain European destinations.

Similar conclusions concerning the relation between unit costs and ship size have also been reached for other products. For example, Figure 6.3 shows the behavior of iron ore and petroleum unit transport costs as one moves from a 20,000-dwt carrier to larger vessels. The greatest unit transport savings occur in the vessel sizes of 25,000 to 50,000 dwt. Thereafter the cost curves flatten out, but the savings continue as the size of the carrier increases to several hundred thousand dwt.

While a full discussion is not possible here, these and other examples show that there is considerable scope for the introduction of cost-saving measures in shipping services supplying developing countries.* However, another factor must be considered along with the adoption of these procedures. This relates to who will in fact benefit from the introduction of these rationalization measures. If shippers, backed by their governments, are not strong enough to negotiate satisfactory agreements with the shipowners, and to ensure that the terms are enforced, then the net result of a rationalization effort could be simply to increase the profits of shipowners. For this reason, it is likely that introduction of cost-saving measures will require complementary government or shippers' council action to ensure an equitable distribution of the benefits.

THE LINER CONFERENCE CODE OF CONDUCT

Developments in international forums also bear on the solution to some developing country transport problems. Specifically, on April 6, 1974, a United Nations Conference of Plenipotentiaries adopted a Code of Conduct for Liner Conferences that represented the

---

*A recent study by W. Prewo and J. Geraci also suggests another line of policy measures that is worthy of further study. Specifically, these authors show that transport elasticities (that is, the ratio of the percentage change in export revenues to the percentage change in freight costs) are frequently greater than unity. It follows that, if these products are characterized by constant or falling returns in production, a combination of transport subsidies and export tax measures may work to the benefit of both domestic exporters and the government.[11]

first attempt at international regulation of this system. As of February 1978, 25 countries, representing approximately 5.7 percent of the world general cargo tonnage, had ratified it.* However, the position of the European Economic Community held the key to success of the Code since it commands a crucial 18 percent of world tonnage and votes as a group. After achieving an internal compromise, the EEC announced in May 1979 its decision to accede to the Code on certain conditions and was followed by other maritime nations. The Code therefore seems likely to gather sufficient support to enter into force, probably in 1981 or 1982.

For most of the countries that participated in formulating the Code as well as those who voted in favor of it, such regulations were thought to be needed to effect the following changes in institutional factors relating to the liner conferences:[12]

- Remove the power to arbitrarily decide on the admission of new lines.
- Provide that the allocation of cargoes within conferences should take place on an internationally agreed basis rather than through the private arrangements by which shares were traditionally determined.
- Bring into the open the levels of conference freight rates and the processes of conference decision taking.
- Restrict the power to take unilateral decisions on matters vitally affecting the trade and economic development of developing countries.
- Establish an independent tribunal to which parties with complaints about the operation of the liner system could have recourse.

Structure of the Code

The Code is divided into seven chapters, containing 54 articles in all, together with an annex consisting of model rules of procedure

---

*It is provided that the Code will enter into force six months after the date on which not less than 24 states, the combined tonnage of which amounts to at least 25 percent of world tonnage, have become contracting parties to it. Article 49 of the Code defines how world tonnage will be interpreted. The number of states required for ratification (24) has not presented a problem but the tonnage condition has. By October 1978, 32 developing countries had become contracting parties to the Convention, but their shipping tonnage was only 5.83 percent of the world fleet.

for international conciliation. Basically, the Code covers two major areas: Chapters III and IV concern the relations between conferences and shippers; while Chapters II and VI deal with relations between member lines within conferences. This latter section contains important provisions for dispute settlement and also provides for a conciliation procedure that is to take precedence over provisions of the domestic law of the states concerned.

The main features of the Code can be summarized as follows: Article 1 acknowledges the right of national lines at either end of a trade route to become members serving that route, and also makes provision for national shipping lines to have equal shares of that trade. Under Article 2, third parties are permitted a "significant portion of the trade," perhaps as much as 20 percent. The recommended breakdown of carriage is, therefore, a 40 percent share for the national lines on the run, with a 20 percent share for outsiders. Thus, the first two articles provide a mechanism whereby national lines can establish themselves in existing conference arrangements with a sizable portion of the trade involved. The measures are also intended to provide a stimulus to investment in developing country national fleets by specifically reserving a large percentage of market shares for these vessels.

Articles 3 and 4 deal with sanctions against members who violate conference rules, establish decision-making procedures, and draw up various self-policing regulations. Article 11 establishes consultation machinery for exporters and conference members. This section of the Code also requires that shippers be given at least 150 days' notification for all general rate increases and stipulates that ten months must elapse between the effective date of one general rate increase and the announcement of another. If a shippers' council feels the proposed rate increase lacks justification, meetings between the liner conference members and exporters are arranged under conditions established in the Code. Procedures are also established for consultation on any bunker or currency surcharges.

Article 8 contains procedural protections for shippers who request dispensations from loyalty arrangements; they are entitled to a prompt decision by the conference on such requests, and also to have the reasons stated in writing if the dispensation is refused. Also, if the conference fails to provide adequate service, shippers can use any available vessel for the carriage of cargo without penalty under any loyalty arrangement.

Article 12 concerns issues relating to freight rates. It requires that in setting rates, account shall be taken of the point that rates "shall be fixed at as low a level as is feasible from the commercial point of view," though they "shall permit a reasonable profit for shipowners." There is no express requirement that freight rates bear some reasonable relation to costs. Article 12 also stipulates that the cost of operations of conferences should, as a rule, be evaluated for the round voyage of ships with the outward and inward directions considered as a single whole.

The other major provision of the Convention relating to the level of freight rates is Article 15, which states that conferences "should" institute promotional rates for nontraditional exports. As noted in Chapter 3 of this book, this article reflects a long-standing demand on the part of developing countries.

Article 18 prohibits predatory practices designed to drive nonmembers out of business. Article 19 declares that conferences must provide "an adequate and efficient service," but there is no indication as to how this will be defined. To draw conference members more closely into the economic affairs of the nations they serve, Article 20 requires that the head offices of shipping enterprises be located in one of the countries involved in a particular trade.

Articles 23 through 46 deal, in detail, with procedural and related requirements for settlement of disputes within conferences; between conferences and shipping lines; between two or more conferences; or between conferences and shippers' councils. The articles also require that conference-shipper disputes be subject to mandatory, but nonbinding, conciliation procedures under the auspices of an international panel of conciliators. Provision is also made for a permanent "registrar" to be established to administer the code's machinery.

The Cargo Reservation Issue

The most notable provision in the Code is Article 2(4), concerning the sharing of conference trade among member lines. There are two basic provisions: first, that in the liner trade between any two states, the national shipping lines of those states shall have "equal right to participate in the freight and volume of traffic generated by their mutual trade"; and second, that third-party lines shall have "the right to acquire a significant part, such as 20 percent, in the freight and volume" of that same traffic. However, the 20 percent figure is not fixed absolutely, it is merely given as an example of what a "significant part" of the trade might be. It is also worth emphasizing that "significant" is the word used, and not "reasonable." Presumably some kind of rule of reason will evolve in practice whereby what is deemed to be "a significant part" of a given conference's trade is settled on the basis of the facts of the particular situation at hand.

It is important to note the distinction between a "national shipping line" and a national-flag line. The former is defined in the Code as "a vessel-operating carrier which has its head office of management and its effective control in that country and is recognized as such by . . . that country. . . ." That is to say, there must be a genuine link between the carrier and the state. Flag of convenience lines will not qualify as national shipping lines. This requirement places a natural limit on the extent to which developing states will be able immediately to increase their share of the world liner traffic at the expense of developed countries. National shipping lines may, however, make use of chartered tonnage.

Notwithstanding all of these points, though, it is clear that the reservation regime of Article 2(4) is intended to bring a major change in the world liner shipping industry. Theoretically, as the national shipping lines of the developing states come to be more and more firmly established, their shares of their relevant conference trades will increase; and the "significant share" allowed to cross traders will correspondingly diminish.

To most efficiency-oriented economists, these cargo reservation provisions are subject to serious reservations since they represent a classic beggar-thy-neighbor device. It has been noted that they do not increase the aggregate trade of the state that passes them, but reallocate trade away from foreigners toward nations. To the extent that this makes shipping more costly, it has been argued that aggregate trade may be reduced.[*] Concerning these objections, Wijkman notes that

> there is little doubt that the cargo reservation formula outlined in the Code is an inappropriate instrument to attain the assumed goals of the Liner Conference Code of Conduct. If its aim is primarily promotional, i.e., to develop merchant marines in developing countries, then direct subsidies to liner companies by governments with maritime ambitions are more efficient. If the aim is primarily regulatory, i.e., to eliminate monopoly profits in international liner shipping, then rate regulation is more efficient and equally feasible. If the aim

---

[*]Neff argues that the cargo subsidy approach is far more preferable as a means of encouraging national fleets since it brings the cost of such operations out into the open and need not have detrimental effects on the overall level of trade.[13]

is to provide a more equitable distribution of income in general or a fairer distribution of tax revenues and rents from an international common property resource, then appropriately designed vessel licensing systems are more efficient. Finally, if the aim is to improve the balance of payments of developing countries, protective measures to promote a domestic merchant marine are appropriate only in exceptional cases.[14]

To a large degree the importance one attaches to these views concerning losses in economic efficiency depends on one's assessment, which must be largely subjective, of the detrimental effects of the current liner system and practices on developing countries' commerce. In opting for cargo reservation and similar policies for encouraging national fleets, it is clear that the developing countries have clearly shown they feel that benefits from increased competitive pressure on the conferences will outweigh any short-term losses due to the competitive advantages cargo reservation conveys on national fleets.

In any overall assessment of the Code a key question concerns the contribution that it will make to redressing developing country grievances concerning institutional factors in shipping. The Code now provides a formal internationally recognized mechanism through which shippers' complaints may be aimed and arbitrated. As such, the true substance and importance of the Code will be determined by the nature of the decisions relating to these disputes as well as by the extent to which members of the international community adhere to the Code's provisions.

NOTES

1. For a more detailed discussion of the policy proposals and specific objectives of the collective self-reliance strategy, see Chapters 2 and 3 in Alexander J. Yeats, Trade and Development Policies: Leading Issues for the 1980s (London: Macmillan, 1981).

2. Wilfred Prewo, "The Structure of Transport Costs on Latin American Exports," Weltwirtschaftliches Archiv 114, no. 2.

3. U. H. Croners, Reference Book for Shippers (New York: Croner Publishers, various issues).

4. See Sidney Dell, A Latin American Common Market? (London: Oxford University Press, 1966), p. 101.

5. Among others, see Joe Bain, "Relation of Profit to Industry Concentration," Quarterly Journal of Economics 65 (August 1951): 297-304; H. M. Mann, "Seller Concentration, Barriers to Entry, and the Rates of Return in Thirty Industries, 1950-60," Review of Economics and Statistics 48 (August 1966):296-307; or Leonard Weiss, "Average Concentration Ratios and Industrial Performance," Journal of Industrial Economics 11 (July 1963):237-54. An excellent summary of the theoretical tie and empirical research on the market structure-performance relationship can be found in F. M. Scherer, Industrial Market Structure and Economic Performance (Chicago: Rand McNally, 1970).

6. See Alexander J. Yeats, "Monopoly Power, Barriers to Competition, and the Pattern of Price Differentials in International Trade," Journal of Development Economics 5 (June 1978):167-80, for evidence on French monopoly pricing practices for exports to their former colonial associates. Perhaps the most comprehensive analysis of the adverse effects of market imperfections on developing countries is the report by G. Helleiner, World Market Imperfections and Developing Countries (Washington, D.C.: Overseas Development Council, 1978).

7. UNCTAD has produced a series of documents concerning establishment of shippers' councils. For one of the most comprehensive, see UNCTAD, Protection of Shippers Interests: Guidelines for Developing Countries (TD/B/C.4/176) (New York: United Nations, 1978).

8. R. Goss, Turnround Time and the Value of Ships Services (Mimeo., no date, p. 15).

9. P. Harff, The Contribution of National Shipping Fleets to the Economic Development of Latin American Countries (in German) (Gottingen: Assen Press, 1970), p. 126.

10. See Stephen Neff, "The UN Code of Conduct for Liner Conferences," Journal of World Trade Law 14 (September-October 1980): 398-415.

11. See W. Prewo and J. Geraci, "Bilateral Trade Flows and Transport Costs," Review of Economics and Statistics 59 (March 1977):67-76.

12. This assessment is from S. G. Sturmey, "The Development of the Code of Conduct for Liner Conferences," Marine Policy 3

(April 1979):139. In a related assessment Per Magnus Wijkman suggests there are three basic objectives of the Code: to increase the
developing countries' share in world liner shipping tonnage to a more
equitable level as part of the New International Economic Order; to
increase the developing countries' share in income generated by world
liner shipping and to redistribute monopoly profits from rich to poor
countries; and to improve developing countries' balance of payments
through substituting domestic shipping services for those under foreign jurisdiction. See Per Magnus Wijkman, Effects of Cargo Reservation: A Review of UNCTAD's Code of Conduct for Liner Conferences
(Stockholm: Institute for International Economic Studies, 1979), p. 4.

13. Neff, "The UN Code."

14. Wijkman, Effects of Cargo Reservation, p. 36.

INDEX

ABOUT THE AUTHOR

ALEXANDER J. YEATS is First Economics Officer with the United Nations Conference on Trade and Development (UNCTAD), Geneva, Switzerland. Previous positions include Visiting Research Fellow at the Institute for International Economic Studies (Stockholm), Ford Foundation Visiting Professor in Turkey, and Research Economist for the Board of Governors of the Federal Reserve Bank in Washington, D.C. He has been on the faculty of the University of Nebraska, the University of Maryland, and Georgetown University.

Dr. Yeats has published over 70 articles in leading economic journals and is the author of two books on trade and development: Trade Barriers Facing Developing Countries and Trade and Development Policies. He was awarded the U.S. National Association of Business Economists' Abramson Prize for outstanding contribution to the field of business economics in 1971-72, and he has served as a consultant to the OECD, the Trilateral Commission, and the Brandt Commission.

Dr. Yeats holds a B.A. in Applied Mathematics from the University of Kansas, an M.A. in Economics from the University of California at Los Angeles, and a Ph.D. in Economics from the University of Nebraska.